DATE DUE

MY 22 '97			
DE 19 '97			
OC 1 02			

DEMCO 38-296

Innovation

Leadership Strategies for
the Competitive Edge

Thomas D. Kuczmarski

Innovation

Leadership Strategies for the Competitive Edge

Printed on recyclable paper

American Marketing Association
Chicago, Illinois

NTC Business Books

NTC a division of *NTC Publishing Group* • Lincolnwood, Illinois USA

Library of Congress Cataloging-in-Publication Data

Kuczmarski, Thomas.
   Innovation : leadership strategies for the competitive edge /
Thomas D. Kuczmarski.
     p.   cm.
   ISBN 0-8442-3324-2
   1. Creative ability in business.   2. Organizational change.
3. New products—Management. I. Title.
   HD53.K834   1995
   658.4'063—dc20   95-11306
                                            CIP
                                         REV.

Published in conjunction with the American Marketing Association,
250 South Wacker Drive, Chicago, Illinois, 60606.

Published by NTC Business Books, a division of NTC Publishing Group
4255 West Touhy Avenue
Lincolnwood (Chicago), Illinois 60646-1975, U.S.A.

56789 BC 987654321

To John, James, and Thomas

contents

Thomas D. Kuczmarski, President of Kuczmarski & Associates, is a nationally recognized expert in new products and services innovation and management, marketing strategy, and growth planning. He has successfully developed new products and business strategies for more than 200 companies in a comprehensive range of industries, from small businesses to *Fortune* 100 corporations.

Before he founded Kuczmarski & Associates more than a decade ago, he was a principal at Booz • Allen & Hamilton, an international management consulting firm. While there, Kuczmarski assisted more than 100 U.S. consumer and industrial goods companies in the areas of marketing, new product development, strategic business analysis, and organizational planning. In addition, he led the firm's in-depth research of the best practices employed by more than 700 U.S. firms in their new product management processes. His prior experience as a brand manager at The Quaker Oats Company also provided a solid and broad-based foundation unique to his consulting specialty.

Kuczmarski's book *Managing New Products: The Power of Innovation* is widely regarded as one of the most comprehensive treatises on developing new products. His newest book, *Values-Based Leadership: Rebuilding Employee Commitment, Productivity and Performance,* is co-authored with Dr. Susan Smith Kuczmarski. He is also extensively published and cited in leading-edge national periodicals. In addition, Kuczmarski is a highly regarded speaker on innovation management and leadership. He lectures nationally and internationally to a broad range of corporations and associations. He is a columnist for *Research & Development* and serves on the editorial review boards for the *Journal of Product Innovation Management* and the *Journal of Consumer Marketing.*

Kuczmarski has been an adjunct professor of new products and services at Northwestern University's Kellogg Graduate School of Management and a lecturer at Columbia University's Executive Management Program in New York. He serves on the boards of Norcross Footwear, Inc. and Kaytee Products, Inc. He is a member of the board of the Chicago Children's Museum and is a member of The Economic Club of Chicago.

He earned an MBA from Columbia University's Graduate School of Business and a master's degree in international affairs from Columbia University's Graduate School of International Affairs, where he was named an International Fellow of the University. He received a BA in French from the College of the Holy Cross and studied at the University of Dijon in France.

WARNING: This book can seriously damage your composure! If you are used to business books that simply offer suggestions on how to run your business, you might find this one too aggressive for your taste. It is written not to instruct, but to challenge your way of thinking and, from there, to change your business mindset.

The subject is innovation, the single most important factor in the future growth of any business venture. The purpose is to jolt senior managers out of their complacency regarding new ideas, new products, and new business strategies. It's time to open your eyes and realize that *you* are either the obstacle or the gatekeeper to the spirit of innovation within your organization.

You bought this book because you are in search of that most elusive of business imperatives, innovation. You've seen stock prices surge as competitors launch a steady stream of successful new products. You've watched from the sidelines as a unique marketing idea or business strategy catapults a rival out of your league into a whole new business ballgame. And now you want to know how you can take your organization there, too.

You know that, contrary to popular belief, new products or new processes alone just won't get you there. What sets truly innovative companies apart is an attitude, a mindset that penetrates every aspect of their business, creating a clear and enduring vision. What you might not realize is that creating and nurturing that mindset within your organization begins and ends with you.

Innovation Succeeds Only If Senior Management Develops the Right Attitude

Innovation cannot be delegated. That's a surefire recipe for failure. Unless top managers consistently and visibly take the lead by championing the spirit of innovation, there is no way it will work.

This book should be read by the management of every enterprise that seeks to innovate, from entrepreneurs and sole proprietors to CEOs, COOs, company presidents, CFOs, CIOs, division or sector presidents, functional vice presidents, senior-level executives, innovation managers, new products directors, and employees at all levels in innovation or new product and service development. More important than holding any of these positions, however, is your attitude toward innovation. You must:

- Believe that innovation has the potential to fuel future profitable growth

- Endorse innovation as a long-term investment rather than a cost that must yield short-term results

- View innovation not as a process or business activity but as a way of thinking, as a mindset that sets you apart from and that will speed you ahead of your competitors

Why I Wrote This Book

I was bitten by the innovation "bug" 20 years ago and have worked with companies to enhance their innovation effectiveness ever since. Throughout that period, I have maintained an intellectual curiosity about and emotional passion for innovation.

I've developed new product strategies, efficient processes, motivating reward systems, dedicated teams, new measurement systems, and radically different and highly innovative new product concepts. I've learned that there is no absolute right way and no absolute wrong way to innovate. Each company has its own identity and challenges, and each works in a different competitive environment. They all, however, share one common characteristic. Top management, particularly the CEO, makes or breaks the spirit of innovation. It's as simple—or complex—as that.

There are four goals this book is intended to achieve:

- Make more CEOs and senior executives believe in the power of innovation to increase earnings, stock price, employee and customer satisfaction, and global competitiveness.
- Increase top management involvement in and commitment to innovation and enhance their understanding of how to capture and cultivate new ideas.
- Unleash the potential of thousands of employees to think more creatively and make innovation happen.
- Provide practical tools, techniques, and guidelines for inspiring innovation and making it work.

It is my hope that when you turn the last pages of this book, you will be as strong a believer as I am that by capturing and cultivating innovative ideas within your organization, you are ensuring its future growth.

Acknowledgments

I would like to thank our many clients, scores of new product practitioners, CEOs, co-workers, and professional colleagues who have provided me with a lifetime laboratory in which I've been able to explore innovation. In particular, I want to express my gratitude to Dr. Susan Smith Kuczmarski, my mentor, values-based partner, friend, and wife, for her consistent support and continued respect. I also want to thank Suzanne Lowe and Meridith Epstein for their significant editorial contributions and advice and my friends and colleagues at Kuczmarski & Associates, from whom I have learned a great deal.

chapter one

What Is Innovation?
The Art of Welcoming Risk

Innovation Defined
According to Webster:
A new idea, method or device; a novelty.

According to Kuczmarski:
A mindset, a pervasive attitude, or a way of thinking focused beyond the present into the future.

The CEO Denial Syndrome

If you are like most CEOs, you are in a state of denial. Most CEOs express a fervent belief in new ideas and claim to be committed to innovation. But actions speak louder than words.

The truth is that most CEOs and senior managers are intimidated by innovation. Viewing it as a high-risk, high-cost endeavor, one that promises uncertain returns, they are afraid to become advocates for innovation. However, because it clearly represents challenge and opportunity, most CEOs deny their reluctance to embrace innovation. They deny that their new product programs are underfunded or understaffed.

They deny that they are closed to new ideas or ways of doing business. They deny that they fail to encourage or reward innovative thinking among their employees. Most of all, they deny that they have created within their organizations a fear of failure that stymies the urge to innovate.

All this denial isn't good. It sends mixed messages throughout the organization and sets up the kind of second-guessing and playing politics that can undermine even the best developed business strategies. Unwilling to be measured by their failures, employees are reluctant to take the risks that the successful development of new ideas demands and, as a result, even the desire to innovate diminishes.

Innovation Principles

This chapter presents five innovation principles that underscore any successful attempt to make innovation happen.

- Innovation is a mindset—a new way to think about business strategies and practice
- Innovation is a key to gaining competitive advantage
- Effective innovation can boost stock price
- CEOs must lead and be held accountable for innovation
- CEOs must be committed to and instill in others a passion for innovation

To adhere to these principles means espousing innovation as a core business strategy. It means accepting that conventional business thinking and practices have not allowed innovation to flourish. Only once old habits are broken and innovation is accepted as a long-term investment can organizations look forward to a future of sustained growth and continued prosperity.

Innovation Is a Mindset

Though you can't touch it, smell it, hear it, see it, or taste it, you *can* sense, think, and feel innovation. Innovation is best described as a pervasive attitude that allows businesses to see beyond the present and create a future vision.

The aspect of innovation that frightens most CEOs is that it is almost always inseparable from risk. Though many pay lip service to the power of innovation, most corporations today are averse to the type of aggressive investment it demands. Instead, they dabble in innovation. They talk about it as the lifeblood of the company and throw occasional resources and R&D dollars into new products development. It's a hot topic in strategic planning meetings. At least one manager or department is charged with "doing" it. But there the commitment usually ends. As most managers discover, it's one thing to talk about innovation, but it's quite another to stake your resources—and your career—on it.

For organizations that *can* change their business mindset, however, and become true innovators, the rewards are tremendous. These organizations begin with a corporate culture that nurtures those who take risks and think creatively, which leads to astonishing growth through radically new products, services, and competitive strategies. This mindset takes time to develop and it rarely thrives without the full and continuing commitment of the company. However, it is not as difficult to cultivate as most believe. Like baking a cake, creating an innovation mindset comes more easily once you have the right recipe. Often, the biggest barrier of all is just not knowing what the key ingredients are. **Exhibit 1.1** provides some insight into how simple the innovation recipe really can be.

Is Innovation Animal, Vegetable, or Mineral?

A blind man is led to an elephant and is asked to determine by touch the species of the animal in front of him. Unable to tell its front from its behind, his reaction is, "This is a large animal with two tails."

Exhibit 1.1

A Recipe for Successful Innovation

Ingredients

- An optimistic, buoyant, and positive CEO
- A commonly agreed-upon new products strategy
- A balanced new product and technology portfolio
- A consumer-driven development process
- Several dedicated teams
- A reward structure for new product participants
- A set of innovation norms and values
- A measurement system for assessing innovation

Directions

Start with a CEO who believes in, conveys optimism about, and consistently commits resources to innovation. Add a new products strategy and technology portfolio. Develop and activate a consumer-driven development process.

Next, mix in several dedicated and upbeat teams of multi-functional members. Motivate them with a reward structure based on performance. Add a set of values and norms for the organization to believe in and act on.

Simmer for approximately five years. Be sure to convey passion and stir regularly. Watch carefully that the innovation mix doesn't burn and keep the heat regulated. Make sure you've already started a new batch before removing the first one from the stove. Assess success by using a previously developed measurement system.

Serves hundreds of thousands of shareholders, employees, and customers. Enjoy!

Like the blind man, most managers are unable to recognize innovation when it is happening right in front of them. Their understanding of what it is and what it involves leaves a lot of room for misinterpretation. Some think of innovation as a broad-ranging creative process, others as simple idea-generation. Some see it as strictly the domain of the new products department, others know it has something to do with marketing, but are not quite sure what. Most just want to get it "done," but fail to devote enough attention or resources to it to make this possible. A few even question whether innovation is important at all.

Is innovation a process? Is it a strategy? Is it a benchmark, a cross-functional team, or a new-to-the-world process? Is innovation a management technique or a leadership responsibility? The answer is that when innovation is done well, it is all of the above and more. A truly innovative organization has developed a mindset that permeates every aspect of its business. There is no halfway measure. That's because innovation is a pervasive attitude, a feeling, an emotional state, an ongoing commitment to newness. It is a set of values that represents a belief in seeing beyond the present and making that vision a reality.

The reason innovation is consistently misunderstood is that for years managers have been focusing on the wrong things. Every year brings new techniques or processes, new organization structures, new research approaches, and, most common of all, new jargon that explains how each of these will stimulate innovation.

But none of these tangible solutions will fix the innovation problem. Innovation is intangible. Intuitive. A state of mind. A pervasive, forward-thinking attitude. Only once companies stop looking for tangible quick-fixes can they develop the mindset that propels and sustains profitable growth.

Innovation Is a Key to Gaining Competitive Advantage

The cost-cutting days are over. We have reengineered, restructured, reorganized, and reexamined ourselves about as much as we can.

Granted, striving to stay cost-competitive is a sound and prudent business practice. However, we have focused too much and far too long on how to become low-cost producers. The incremental benefit of streamlining our processes, reducing our work force, and decreasing our unit costs (in most cases) is limited.

It's time to take some calculated risks and to view innovation as the Bank of Tomorrow. Make deposits into it today, and it will yield dividends in the future. It's time to stop focusing on the cost side of the business success equation and turn to the demand side. Stimulating demand is far more difficult than cutting costs. It is also far more rewarding.

To gain real competitive advantage, the focus of innovation must be on developing new-to-the-world or new-to-the-market products that provide consumers with totally new perceived benefits. Too frequently, the results of innovation are two types of new products:

1. "Me-too" products (improved versions of existing products).
2. "Trend-of-the-moment" products like "clear" products, "natural," "single-serving" sizes, new colors, and "in" flavors.

The unfortunate outcome of these types of new products is usually low financial returns and a relatively short life. Truly innovative and radically new products are the ones that competitors lose sleep over, and with good reason. They have staying power and profit-making stamina.

Innovation is the single best way to leapfrog competition, move ahead of the industry pack, and, most important, create new ways to bolster profit margins and fuel future earnings streams. What more could you possibly ask? If it's done right, innovation can be your most powerful competitive weapon. As a CEO of a $500 million manufacturing firm reminds us,

I got tired of trying to play catch-up all the time with my competitors. Now the tables have turned. The past five new products we launched have them scrambling.

Effective Innovation Can Boost Stock Price

Isn't the primary goal of every CEO to increase shareholder wealth and generate higher returns to the owners of the company? You bet it is. One of the fastest ways to achieve stock price appreciation is to launch a steady stream of competitive successful new products and services. The key here, of course, is *successful* new innovations. The introduction of failures or new and improved line extensions won't yield increased quarterly dividends or attract new investors. But effective innovations will.

Companies like Rubbermaid, 3M, Apple, and Kellogg have gained a reputation as innovators. They view new products as the central core of their business strategies, not merely a peripheral exercise. They work at innovation, are committed to it, and enjoy consistent financial rewards from it. Their stock price appreciation from the mid-1970s to the mid-1990s reflects it.

The major reason many initial public offerings (IPOs) experience rapid and significant stock price escalation is that they offer investors something *new*. Witness the incredible stock price surges of Boston Market, Petsmart, and Starbucks Coffee. Each has more than doubled in share price since its initial offering—not a bad return for an investor. Why did their prices go through the roof? Because they offer new benefits to consumers. Consumers have always been able to go to retail stores and purchase chicken, pet foods, and coffee. Kentucky Fried Chicken, the local independent pet store, and Chock Full O' Nuts have offered these products for years. So what's so new?

- Boston Market offers a "healthy," "home-cooked" alternative to fried chicken.
- Petsmart provides a one-stop shopping benefit with a wide range of product offerings for your pet.
- Starbucks offers a wide range of coffee flavors and styles in an upscale environment, a combination that enables consumers to experience coffee, not just drink it.

Consequently, shareholders are recognizing the benefits of and rewarding the results of innovation. Sometimes a single new product can fuel stock price. This is certainly the case with many telecommunications firms and biotechnology companies. The announcement of AVONEX's clinical test results by Biogen increased the stock price more than 15 share points in one day. Motorola's introduction of cellular phones has served as a stock price lever for years.

Whether it's a steady stream of new products, a new innovative company, or even a big-hit new product success, shareholders are getting smarter. They do understand the power of innovation. It's time for CEOs to mirror their insight. It's time for senior managers to put innovation at the very top of their "to-do" lists.

CEOs Must Lead and Be Held Accountable for Successful Innovation

CEOs will agree that they are each responsible for setting the strategic course and guiding the future profitable growth of their company. This usually means developing the right strategy, allocating the appropriate mix of resources, leading the organization, and ensuring a steady and consistent stream of earnings. The attainment of strategic and financial goals set for the company is usually the top priority of the CEO. It is the ball that most CEOs keep their eyes focused on.

Coaching for Innovation

With the right team in place, innovation becomes the energy source to tackle the competition, score a touchdown, and win the game. An innovation mindset, in effect, is the training ground for a winning team. It ensures that there is a solid foundation on which to build future successes. The irony, then, is that many CEOs spend more time worrying about the financial community's reaction to a quarterly earnings report than about how to support innovation. That's the same as the coach worrying about the press conference after the game is lost.

Instead, smart coaches train, motivate, and guide their players before the game. They instill in the team a spirit, a belief, and a passion. Coaches make players feel confident and help them to believe in themselves. Coaches prepare players to develop a winning mindset. Calling the right plays is important, but strategies are not worth much if you don't pick the best players, practice, and motivate the team to think "win." A winning innovation team combines strategy and implementation to beat the competition time after time.

Innovation at the Center

A company must have innovation as the core of its business strategy. Marketing strategies, capital investments, manufacturing plans, and R&D expenditures must be developed, built, and allocated around innovation—not the other way around. Develop strategic roles for innovation that you'll want new products to satisfy. Link the role of innovation integrally to the business strategy. Don't tack on new products as an addendum to the strategic business plan. Rather, position innovation as the centerpiece; make it the heart and soul of the growth strategy. Make innovation the primary tool for hammering out a strategy for tomorrow. Innovation is not one more thing to get done. Instead, it should be viewed as a way of life—a new way of thinking, managing, and feeling.

Who better to guide the future and growth of a company than its senior management? And what's better suited to achieve successful growth than innovation? There are few responsibilities embraced by a senior manager that are more vital than innovation. Capturing an innovation mindset, and, in turn, instilling it, is the starting point for activating a successful pipeline of new products.

CEOs must serve as the catalyst for sparking an innovation mindset throughout a company. This responsibility cannot be delegated. It must be the leadership responsibility of any CEO. Compensation should be directly impacted by the rise or fall of successful innovation. CEOs should be held accountable by their boards of directors, and ultimately by their shareholders, for the achievement of an innovation mindset and the resultant fruits of innovation. Many other key players make up the innovation team, but the ultimate responsibility for innovation lies with the CEO.

CEOs Must Be Committed to and Instill in Others a Passion for Innovation

Sending out a flurry of memos about innovation won't cut it. A passion for innovation must be inculcated within the hearts and minds of senior management before it can permeate an organization. Innovation can't merely receive an occasional mention or occasional surges of additional resources. Senior management must believe in innovation and tout it as the most valuable strategic advantage that the company could ever hope to achieve. Actions must support the words. A fervor for and intensity about innovation must be conveyed.

Passion means emotion. A commitment to innovate cannot be conveyed through a dry corporate dictum like, "We will become more innovative." Rather, it requires a heartfelt and consistent belief that innovation can make a difference. CEOs need, first, to believe in it, then to convince their employees that they believe it.

Fostering an Innovation Mindset

An innovation mindset in one person can gradually be transmitted to an entire organization. You know a company with an innovation mindset when you see the way employees interact with one another. They treat one another with respect, admiration, and cooperation. They smile. They laugh. They express consideration and thoughtfulness. They listen. They focus on the benefits desired by consumers rather than on their own personal gain. They come to work with an optimistic enthusiasm, because they believe that what they do each day really does count. They focus on the future rather than on the past. They exude self-confidence, possess a healthy self-esteem, and believe in their own capabilities and strengths. They have faith in innovation and in each other.

Transcending Levels and Functional Areas

An innovation mindset is an attitude that should be adopted throughout an organization by virtually every employee, from the CEO to hourly workers. It is a pervasive spirit that stimulates individuals, as well as teams, to holistically endorse a belief in creating newness across all dimensions of the company:

- New markets
- New product ideas
- New manufacturing approaches
- New customer segments
- New selling methods
- New people
- New businesses
- New strategic directions
- New ways to deliver old products
- New services
- New leadership constructs
- New research techniques
- New thinking
- New adaptations
- New improvements to existing products

- New pay on performance compensation systems
- New ways to measure innovation

Passion for Innovation Begins with You

Achieving a far-reaching innovation mindset—one that permeates every leader and employee—is not easy. How can a CEO or vice president ever hope to infuse an innovation mindset? Unfortunately, most don't even try. Not because they don't recognize the importance of innovation, but rather because they become discouraged. They don't feel inspired themselves. Self-commitment is the first requirement, once the importance of and benefits from innovation are recognized. Then they need to understand how best to convey that inspiration, passion, and belief in innovation to the rest of the organization. Senior managers need to develop a passion for innovation and then transfer that mindset to their innovation teams.

Is innovation a critical component to your company's future growth and profitability? In most cases, the answer is yes. Is your company successful at innovation? Does the CEO talk up the need for and benefits of innovation? Do people get rewarded for successful innovation? Do most employees have an innovation mindset? In most cases, the answer to these questions is no.

If innovation is so important, then why don't more senior managers pay closer attention to it, provide the talent required, pony up the investment dollars, and become more involved? Maybe it's fear. Maybe it's due to a short-term focus. Keep in mind, the typical *Fortune* 500 CEO is only in office, on average, for 6.5 years. And the financial community is demanding increased earnings every 90 days.

If an innovation mindset is embodied in the soul of only one manager, a seed for innovation has been planted. But creating newness most often stems from the collective skills, creativity, insights, and values of many people. While creative individuals exist in many organizations, radical innovation occurs, for the most part, through the efforts of motivated teams, task forces, and committees. In short, motivated and effectively managed groups of people make innovation happen.

But groups need to be led, to have a reason to believe, and to be effectively managed and motivated. Now we're back to the hard part. A new incentive plan, organizational shift, or new hire will not an innovation mindset make. That's been the problem for years. Managers jump from one new fad to the next. These Band-Aid solutions don't work. Discouraged and continually frustrated, managers abandon innovation and focus on things they can get their hands and heads around: reducing costs, redesigning processes, acquiring companies, and increasing market share of existing businesses. The price they pay is the opportunity to innovate.

Management Wants Innovation But Doesn't Know How to Create It

Some executives espouse a belief that innovation is a major factor in creating competitive advantage for their organizations and can serve as the fuel for future growth. Yet U.S. business is still struggling to develop a successful approach for effectively managing innovation.

Management continuously seeks ways to deploy limited capital and human resources toward implementing the firm's innovation goals, but they do not know the following:

- How to relate innovation to their corporate goals and strategy
- How to organize, compensate, and motivate innovation managers
- How to allocate resources and make innovation investments
- How to measure their return on innovation investments

Too often, the task of developing new products is delegated to middle-level management ranks simply because senior managers are not knowledgeable about the whole process of innovation and new product development. Beyond that, they are uncomfortable with the very concept of innovation. Many view new product development as a necessary evil. They think of innovation as a profit-eating monster rather than a growth- and earnings-yielding investment. For most senior managers, risk aversion is the sand that slows the wheels of innovation.

The importance of innovation has not, however, dwindled away. On the contrary, its role in providing companies with a competitive edge in the marketplace is increasingly recognized. The need for innovation leadership has arrived.

Permission to Fail

Quantity counts. Successful innovation comes only after many attempts, with simultaneous development initiatives underway, and after failures have been experienced. Granted, there are techniques and proven methodologies that can provide a new products team with assistance and guidance. But knowledge and application of these techniques alone will not guarantee new product winners and innovation success. Analogous to the accomplished artist who discards many attempts on canvas, even experienced new products managers have many false starts, failures, and only partially finished innovation endeavors. Yes, some big new product successes are achieved, but many failures are also strewn along the path to success.

When one stops to think about the total number of works that an artist initiates in a lifetime, the quantity is mind-boggling. Picasso reportedly sketched or painted more than 10,000 works. That's about the same number as all new products launched in grocery retail stores in any one year. Picasso continued to paint into his 90s but discarded about two out of every three of his canvases. That translates to about a 33 percent success rate.

However, for some reason, nobody ever thinks about Picasso's "failures." People instead stand in awe of his artistic successes. In contrast, most senior executives focus their attention on new product failures, cycle time reduction, improving efficiency, and reducing new product costs and allocated resources. Why don't they rather applaud and celebrate the new product successes? Are there too few of them? Is one creative endeavor each year inadequate? How much is enough? Perhaps they just don't recognize that failures are inherent to and part of innovation. It's impossible to generate a 100 percent success rate. This fact must become a core component of an innovation mindset. Failures must accompany successes. Companies must understand that while some of their efforts will yield winners, others won't.

Consequently, the right way for CEOs to judge innovation results is in terms of the portfolio of new products and services launched over a defined period—often five years. There are two important elements of this attitude: the portfolio perspective and the five-year horizon.

The Portfolio Perspective

Successful new products managers will perceive innovation as a portfolio of different types of new products with varying degrees of risk, potential return upside, and strategic roles. Think of innovation performance like a stock portfolio. In any group of stocks the investor will experience some individual losers, but as long as the portfolio is increasing in value by 15–20 percent per year, the investor is able to claim that a successful investment strategy has been designed and implemented.

CEOs must stop obsessing about new product failures. Similar to a stock portfolio, every new products portfolio will include failures. The issue is whether or not the overall group of new products is yielding adequate financial returns over time and satisfying strategic roles, all of which help the business to achieve its long-term goals.

The Five-Year Horizon

The second part of this attitude is measuring the performance of the new products portfolio over a five-year period. Unless we're dealing with a fad product, like a new type of bubble gum, new products usually take several years to develop and a couple of more years before they become profitable. That's why a continuous stream of new product launches is imperative. Without seamless innovation, which continues consistently over time, one can't expect innovation results to be positive. A jolt or infusion of innovation won't turn a failing new products portfolio into a successful one. It takes time. And quantity does count.

Measuring the Consistency of Your Innovation Message

It's critical for senior managers to monitor themselves to make sure that their words are supported by their actions. Inconsistencies between words and actions send out mixed signals. They confuse and demoralize employees. They hear one thing and see another. They start trying to second-guess what your words really mean. They anticipate your future actions, which will be different from what you're saying today.

Take your own pulse on how well your actions support your words. Often your intentions are good, but there are many different conflicts and trade-off decisions that influence your ability to behave in ways that reinforce your oral or written statements. The following are ways CEOs can support their verbal commitment to innovation:

- Send out an article that discusses innovation.
- Send memos out to new product team members congratulating them on a job well done.
- Schedule time to attend some new product team meetings.
- Hold an awards banquet recognizing the top performing new product teams during the past year.

- Send new product team leaders on a cruise with their spouses.
- Tell the financial community about the role innovation will play in the future growth strategy.
- Put in place a new compensation system to motivate new product teams.
- Avoid cutting the innovation budget.

Knowing how to create an innovation mindset is, of course, what this book is all about. But it is first essential for you to become a believer in innovation. If you choose, however, to pursue a different direction—one that minimizes or doesn't include innovation—that's fine. Just make sure that you've clearly communicated that strategy to your employees. There's nothing more frustrating for employees than to spin their wheels on innovation activities, only to learn after months or years that senior management isn't all that committed to it. However, if innovation is important to your company, you need to get yourself in a positive frame of mind about it. The cost-cutting days are fading. It's the dawn of innovation.

Innovation Insights

Many personal discoveries have emerged over the last 20 years since I've been involved with innovation. I have found that most of these observations are applicable to any kind of company: big or small; manufacturer or service provider; hi-tech or low-tech; emerging markets or mature markets; and consumer, industrial, or business-to-business. My top ten innovation insights follow:

1. **Failure is an intrinsic part of innovation.** Even successful new product companies experience a 35 percent failure rate of commercialized new products. CEOs who accept this, understand this, and promulgate an attitude that allows risk-

taking will be the victors. Mistakes will be made. Willingness to accept some failures will inculcate confidence in new product participants and over time generate higher financial results.

2. **Companies that have a new products strategy in place are more successful.** By identifying the financial goals, strategic roles, and screening criteria that new products should satisfy, innovation is positioned within a strategic and business context. This forms a bridge to the Island of Innovation. The new product initiatives underway have a strategic anchor that grounds them in business reality. The new products strategy links innovation efforts to the long-range plan for the business. Goals are complementary to, not in conflict with, the existing business and new product objectives.

3. **Using multi-functional teams with dedicated team members is critical for success.** You can't develop radically new products while simultaneously putting out fires on the existing business. The opposing responsibilities between new products and the existing business will result in new products playing second fiddle. Appoint people to focus on, become immersed in, and be surrounded by innovation. This way, they will have the time, concentration, and motivation to develop an innovation mindset.

4. **A systematic, well-defined, and commonly understood new product development process is a given—not a differentiator for successful innovation.** Without a widely accepted process, don't even attempt to undertake innovation. However, even with a clear process, there are many other variables that drive innovation effectiveness. Process is a necessary enabler, but alone it just won't spur innovation.

5. **Compensation incentives that simulate an entrepreneurial environment are more likely to motivate participants on new products and innovation teams.** Enabling new products people to win big or lose big, depending on the

financial performance of new products, provides a financial motivational factor. I've seen many different types of incentives work and have created an array of different approaches that companies have used, ranging from new product stock options to $75,000 bonuses per team member. If an eight-person new products team generates a $10 million new product that drops 12 percent to the bottom line and continues to grow for five years, is there anything wrong with giving them 10 percent of the incremental earnings? Remember, the company keeps 90 percent of the incremental profits generated.

6. **Top management commitment is the foundation on which successful innovation is built.** I've seen this factor alone be the tie-breaker between success and failure. There are three ingredients to top management commitment: (1) allocation of adequate financial resources, including R&D and technology funds, and assigning some of the best people to new products; (2) a perspective that allows for failures, mistakes, and a long-term payback from the investments being made into the innovation "bank"; and (3) an expressively proactive, positive, "can-do," "I-believe-in-you" attitude.

7. **Companies that are successful innovators keep track of their results and know how much bang they are getting for their innovation buck.** Over a five-year period, they monitor and record success rates, investment levels, survival rates, financial performance, and returns from each new product launched as well as the total portfolio of new products. They stay on top of new product expenditures and assess their returns on innovation. They recalibrate future investments and fine-tune return expectations annually.

8. **Developing a portfolio of new product types helps to diversify risk and provide a balanced investment approach to innovation.** Over a five-year period, a company should aim to have at least one-third of its new product successes be new-

to-the-world, truly innovative new products. This is hard to do. There is a natural tendency toward the quicker, lower-risk new product types like line extensions, new and improved versions, and repositionings. Over time, investing in a diversified new products portfolio increases the risk/return ratio.

9. **Companies should begin the new product development process with customer problem identification and need intensity research.** Don't start the development process with idea generation. The right approach to making innovation happen is to view it as creative problem solving—not blue-sky brainstorming. The difference is distinct. By taking a look first at consumer-identified problems, hassles, gripes, complaints, and unmet needs, idea generation can then be aimed at creating new solutions to resolve, address, or improve them. A problem-solving framework focuses idea generation in a way that results in higher-potential new product ideas. Besides, consumers can't really articulate what new products they'd like. However, they can describe to you, crisply and clearly, things they dislike and activities, events, and situations that cause them problems that produce new needs.

10. **Identify innovation values and new product team norms to guide behavior and communications among team members.** You must determine individual team member goals, hopes, fears, and aspirations. You need to have each individual member discuss with the entire team his or her reasons for participating in the development of new products. Each one of them should articulate what he or she wants to get out of it—personally. What are their real motivations for being involved with innovation? What will turn them off? What are they scared of, as they embark on this adventure? Companies that allow teams to invest adequate time up front to do this, and are open to the inputs made, help to solidify and empower new product teams. This coalesces the people power that usually lies dormant within a team.

Is Innovation an Art or a Science?

During the first half of the 1990s, innovation has emerged again as an acceptable and desired route to growth. Perhaps the acquisitions pipeline has dried up or downsizing mania has caused senior executives to better utilize precious people resources. Yet many executives today, similar to myself 20 years ago, haven't figured out how to create an environment that breeds innovation.

Innovation is not a science. Innovation is an art. You can tell if a new product or service will be a success or failure only after it has been completed and launched into the marketplace. Its success is then determined by consumers, who judge its value or worth based on their own criteria.

Likewise, an artist cannot tell when sitting down to paint whether a particular piece of art will end up as a masterpiece. Even if the artist believes it is a great piece of work, its value or "success" will ultimately be determined by the art collectors who will judge its quality.

The same is true of innovation. A new products manager cannot sit down and merely say, "I'm now going to create a $5 million new product success." Successful innovation comes with practice. It requires a lot of hard work. It comes from an intrinsic belief that persistent attempts will eventually generate successful new products. The belief in one's ability to innovate must be steadfast, consistent, and deep. That's why innovation is a mindset rather than a series of sequential activities. It requires an attitude of positive self-esteem. It supports a buoyant and optimistic belief that, over time, innovation will result.

The Rush to Failure

Too often, a company begins its new product development effort by just digging in and transforming a great new idea into a prototype that can quickly be test-marketed. Worse yet, top management will insist, "Let's get that new product idea out the door by next quarter."

The major disadvantage of this approach is that although it might work well once, on average it will contribute to nothing more than a series of new product fits and starts. Speed-to-market success at the risk of sacrificing quality will not yield positive long-term results.

The key to new product success is treating it as a key component of business strategy. Effective innovation is not a creative, unstructured brainstorming activity. Rather, it is a multidisciplinary function and a deliberate investment in a company's future. Innovation should never be viewed as a cost center. It is by its very nature a long-term investment.

Coincident with this thinking is the need for top management to accept the uncertainty and inherent risk of new products. New product failures are unavoidable. In fact, they are a key part of the success formula. Failures provide new lessons from which to learn. They need to be examined, and new insights that surface from them should be integrated into the process. Go ahead and make changes to the way you do innovation as long as they are based on an experiential rationale.

In working with scores of companies to develop new product programs, I find, time and again, several factors that distinguish winning innovators from their "not so lucky" counterparts. Unfortunately, innovation success cannot be achieved through "black box" magic. Waving a magic wand will not transform a new product toad into a prince. However, viewing innovation as a source of competitive advantage can have a huge impact on turning your company into a profitable and growing entity.

To See Beyond and Act upon It

Senior executives need to be actively involved in setting the mindset, direction, and environment for innovation. In your role as business strategy leader, you need to cast innovation as the protagonist in your company's scenario of future growth.

You need to instill a confidence in your people that enables them to see beyond the present and develop a vision of the future. To see beyond today's service offerings to totally new-to-the-world services. To see beyond the current business paradigm to a more effective future paradigm. To see beyond the predictable to the imagined. To see beyond today's definition of the business to a more expansive business definition that includes new benefits to customers.

Carl Bochmann, a former senior partner at Booz • Allen & Hamilton, now vice president of Riverbend Engineering in Cleveland, Ohio, serves on the editorial board of the *Journal of Product Innovation Management*. He has spent nearly 30 years developing new products and helping companies to achieve and plan for successful innovation. In 1994, he wrote me a letter about some of his thoughts on innovation mindsets:

> The innovator has a vision, assumes the vision will be realized, and sets a course to that vision. The innovator's understanding of the present is no less accurate or realistic than others; but acceptance of the predictable and expected outcome is unthinkable. The innovator assumes the vision is inevitable and then interpolates events, activities and requirements between the present and the envisioned future. The innovator does not dwell on incremental steps, rather the innovator starts with a quantum leap. The innovator cannot extrapolate because extrapolation is founded on the past and limited by irrelevant prior boundaries.
>
> It is important to note that the innovative mindset is unique or identifiable only in the penchant for seeing beyond what is and focusing on what might be. Except for this characteristic, the innovator may exhibit a broad array of thought processes; from realistic to optimistic, subjective to objective, linear to circular or algorithmic to heuristic. The innovator is no dreamer locked into a fantasy world. Quite the opposite, the innovator probably sees beyond what exists today because of a realistic appraisal of the need for improvements tomorrow.
>
> And it is precisely this forward thinking attitude that *can* be ingrained in the culture of an organization to create the innovative and dynamic enterprise that we all admire so much when we see it.

Innovation is the ability to look forward, to exude a passion about the future, to be curious, to be a contrarian, and to think about the present from different perspectives. But cultivating the capability to do this, that is, to achieve an innovation mindset, requires time, patience, information, and a desire to discover.

Thomas Edison and Christopher Columbus had an innovation mindset. Stan Gault, Steven Jobs, and Lee Iacocca also have demonstrated innovation mindsets. Anita Roddick and Howard Schultz have innovation mindsets. Each of their discoveries provided us with new goods or services that others around them never uncovered. The electric light bulb, the New World, Rubbermaid products, Apple Computer, the mini-van, the Body Shop, and Starbucks are all the result of braving an innovation mindset.

Amazingly, in the late 1800s, the United States Patent Office almost closed down because government officials believed that all possible innovations had already been invented. Fortunately, they were persuaded to leave it open for a few more years—just to be sure!

Likewise, back in the late 1970s, I remember having a discussion with a new products manager in a major telecommunications firm who assured me that the innovation game had reached maturity in this industry. His mindset was clearly not an innovative one. Soon after came the birth of cellular phones, fax machines, automated teller machines, call forwarding, and scores of other major telecommunications innovations. The key is not to think in the present or ponder the past. The right approach is to think about what could be in the future.

The Four Daily Requirements for CEOs to Instill Innovation

In order to create an innovation mindset and culture within an organization, there are a few things senior managers should remember, think about, and act on each and every day. Keeping innovation top-of-mind is crucial. Following the four daily requirements will help foster the right mindset to support effective innovation.

Trust Your Teams and Functional Managers

Once you've formed new product teams, trust them, empower them, and stay committed to them. Employees are fragile. You can easily fragment them and leave them demoralized, disjointed, and dysfunctional. Instead, you need to convey a strong belief in your new product teams and the functional managers with whom they interact. A conviction and trust that they can feel. A fervent and passionate belief that they will be able to identify, create, and develop a portfolio of successful new products and services.

Ensure Recognition, Rewards, and Respect

Convey respect to the people that are trying to cope with the demands, frustrations, and anxieties caused by working in the discipline of innovation. Respect their dedication, fortitude, and prodigious work. Respect their intelligence, creativity, and analytics. Respect their judgment and intuition. Respect their experience.

Be sure to recognize their efforts, small triumphs, and major accomplishments. Write them notes, convey thanks, and express appreciation for their initiatives. Reward them with descriptive praise and ensure that you keep your word with high financial rewards once they've launched profitable new innovation successes.

Be Positive, Buoyant, and Supportive

The way in which you express positive support to new product teams and functional managers will be instrumental in motivating them. The feedback you give them must be genuine and sincere. Some constructive criticism and additive thinking can be beneficial once in a while. For the most part, though, you need to be the inspiring and motivational coach. Be buoyant and uplifting. Make your new product teams feel proud to be working on innovation. Help each individual to see how his or her job plays a major role in contributing to overall innovation success.

Don't Cut the Funding

Although you'll often think about cutting the budget, people resources, and research investments, don't. Just don't. And don't let your board of directors or executive committee convince you differently. Fight for it. Stick to your guns. Don't loosen your grip on maintaining it. Reinforce in your own mind daily that innovation is a long-term adventure, not a short-term exercise. Bolster your own belief in the benefits of innovation and tell yourself that this is an investment that you can't withdraw. The penalties will be severe if you do. You can't afford to "cash in."

Innovation Checklist: Innovation Insights

1. Accept failure as an intrinsic part of innovation.
2. Develop a new products strategy.
3. Establish multi-functional teams with dedicated members.
4. Define a systematic new products development process.
5. Design compensation incentives that simulate an entrepreneurial environment.
6. Foster top management commitment to innovation.
7. Track the results of innovation efforts.
8. Develop a balanced portfolio of new product types to diversify risk.

9. Identify customer problems and needs before generating new product ideas.

10. Define new product team values and norms to guide behavior and communications.

chapter two

Innovation Strategy
The Power of Competitive Advantage

As America's economy slips further into the doldrums, innovation is beginning to be recognized as a national priority.

—Rosabeth Moss Kanter, *The Change Masters*

The Strategic Power of Innovation

Innovation has been overlooked and neglected for years by many companies as a key component of business strategy. For too long, the primary thrust of strategic thinking and planning has centered on how best to become low-cost producers. Of course, reducing costs and increasing operating efficiencies are important pieces of any smart business strategy puzzle. But innovation brings with it far more potential power to reach strategic and financial business goals. The role of innovation in setting and bolstering strategy has not been well understood or accepted in the past. However, signs of support for innovation are definitely being seen in corporations. CEOs are turning to innovation as a growth mode for adding incremental revenues and profits to their income statement. But, many still don't think about innovation as a core business strategy.

Every CEO should seriously consider innovation as a competitive weapon for shaping business strategies. For many years, CEOs and strategic planners have used Michael Porter's model for setting competitive strategy. Although there are excellent aspects to this model, its major flaw is its neglect of innovation. Innovation can be inferred as the approach to achieve some of the strategies using Porter's model, but it's never singled out on its own as a core business strategy. It should be. Choosing among product differentiation, low-cost producer, or segment focus are all smart strategic options. However, innovation should be included in this set of alternatives for growing a profitable business.

Consequently, CEOs should look at innovation as the major source for building competitive advantage over a future five-year period. "Competitive innovation" should become a new term in the strategic planning lexicon. We need to change the way we think about strategy and the way we manage risk. Too many CEOs manage risk according to the potential downside impact rather than envisioning the upside potential of taking innovation risks. Innovation can provide the power to propel a company ahead of its competition, and it offers an avenue to growth that can be grounded in long-term competitive advantage.

So the issue here is not to present a case that competitive innovation is better than a low-cost producer strategy, but rather to propose that competitive innovation is an equally appealing alternative for building strategic power. Another important element of competitive innovation is that it can be used as a business strategy to help protect, defend, and grow existing product lines, as well as serve as a growth mode for expanding and diversifying into new product or business areas. When many companies evaluate their core competencies, they tend to assess their sources of competitive advantage according to some of the following areas:

- Manufacturing economies
- R&D technology
- Channel clout
- Brand name equity
- Distribution leverage
- Price competitiveness

The smart executive of the future should assess one more source of competitive advantage—that is, the company's potential for achieving competitive innovation.

The Two "Power" Roles of Innovation

Senior executives should think of innovation as a valuable corporate asset rather than a cost or a risk. If you truly perceive innovation as a source of competitive advantage, it will more likely be viewed as a long-term investment rather than a short-term cost. This long-term investment perspective sets up the right mindset for innovation to work effectively. Without it, innovation is perceived as a high risk. And as a consequence, your managers will take the low-risk approach of merely cutting costs or focusing on line extensions and product improvements.

Broadly speaking, there are two key power roles that innovation can play: (1) competitive advantage protection (CAP), which stems from competitive innovation, and (2) shareholder, employee, and customer (SEC) satisfaction. The first, competitive advantage protection, provides a company with a long-term competitive "insurance" policy. Most importantly, it allows a company to play an offensive game in the marketplace rather than a reactionary game of always trying to catch up to competition.

Competitive Advantage Protection

Let's define this new term so we're clear on its meaning:

> **Competitive advantage protection:** A strategic approach for preempting, protecting against, or jumping ahead of competition. Competitive advantage protection enables a company to accelerate growth, experience incremental margin enhancement, and build additional core competency, which bolsters competitive advantage.

Exhibit 2.1 graphically depicts the role that competitive advantage protection can play in shaping business strategy. In each quadrant, competitive advantage protection can play a significant role in enhancing competitive advantage. Each of the quadrants is described here:

1. **Radical Leapfrogging.** With this strategy, competitive advantage protection is aimed at achieving new products that will leapfrog competition. The end outputs of this strategy usually are products or services that convey totally new consumer-perceived benefits. They are radically different from anything currently offered in the market. Consumers or end-users will clearly perceive the functional, emotional, psychological, or performance benefits of these new products as better or greater than those offered by any competitive product.

2. **Benefits Differentiation.** Competitive innovation can play a major role in adding new benefits to an existing product. By focusing on new benefits, the existing or newly developed product will provide a new source for competitive advantage.

The degree of uniqueness and benefit differentiation will most likely determine the duration and strength of the competitive advantage.

3. **Market Share Stimulation.** There are many different approaches for stimulating market share, ranging from advertising and promotions to distribution channel diversification and pricing. However, competitive innovation can also be used to build market share by launching line extensions, flankers, and new-and-improved products. This approach offers end-users new reasons to purchase your product line rather than your competition's.

4. **Cost/Value Enhancement.** Value-engineering or cost-reduced new products and processes can also be achieved through competitive innovation. Sometimes the lower cost benefit can be passed on directly to consumers, resulting in a price reduction. Alternatively, the cost savings can be applied internally to boost gross profit margins. These incremental margin dollars can then be used to build awareness or stimulate trial through increased marketing.

The key point of this framework is to heighten the awareness of competitive advantage protection to strategy makers, and then have them view it as a key strategic lever for building future competitive advantage. CEOs should put the risk aspect of innovation in the right perspective: High returns from innovation can only be achieved through pursuit of higher-risk forms of innovation, such as radically new products and products that offer totally new benefits. As a billion-dollar company's CEO said,

The R&D investments I'm making today will bear fruit for my successor. They will enable the new CEO to pass by our competition with innovative new products which the competition won't be able to duplicate for a while.

Exhibit 2.1

Competitive Advantage Protection

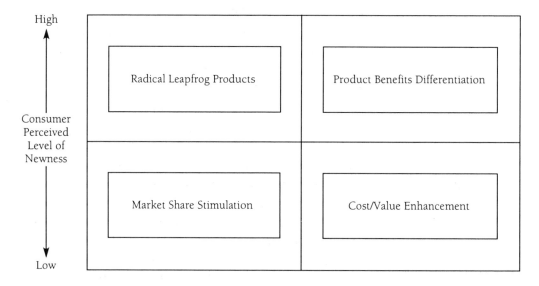

	High	
	Radical Leapfrog Products	Product Benefits Differentiation
Consumer Perceived Level of Newness		
	Market Share Stimulation	Cost/Value Enhancement
	Low	

Shareholder, Employee, Customer Satisfaction

The second power role, shareholder, employee, customer (SEC) satisfaction, provides a means for increasing the satisfaction level of companies' three key constituencies. If satisfaction can be increased for these constituencies with increased profitability, it's fairly safe to assume that the senior management will be rewarded handsomely.

Executives should adopt a new mindset regarding these three constituencies. This shareholder-employee-customer triumvirate should represent the collective group that executives are trying to best serve. The leader of an organization becomes a servant whose primary job is to satisfy the needs, expectations, and desires of this collective group. The three constituencies fall on a continuum, from externally to internally focused, as shown in **Exhibit 2.2.**

Exhibit 2.2

Innovation Focus

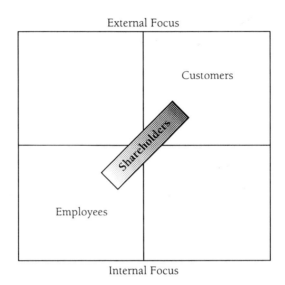

External Focus

Customers

Shareholders

Employees

Internal Focus

Senior management must satisfy all three of these constituencies simultaneously over time. Satisfaction levels of each might fluctuate from time to time, but managers should seek a balanced approach aimed at satisfying all three. The measures of satisfaction for each should be kept relatively simple, and the measurement criteria should be customized on a company-specific basis. An illustrative set of SEC satisfaction criteria is shown in **Exhibit 2.3.**

By developing successful new products and services that drop incremental profit dollars to the bottom line by satisfying customers' needs and wants, all three constituencies can be served. There is no CEO alive who isn't interested in accomplishing the two roles—CAP and SEC satisfaction—that I've proposed for innovation. All CEOs should want to increase the satisfaction of shareholders, employees, and customers

Exhibit 2.3

SEC Satisfaction Criteria

Shareholders

- Stock price goes up 15 percent annually
- Dividends increase every other quarter

Employees

- Pride in company deepens
- Bonuses increase annually
- Careers advance
- Compensation accelerates by more than 10 percent annually
- Job security solidifies
- Personal satisfaction from job is enhanced

Customers

- Products satisfy needs and solve problems
- Products offer benefits that exceed competitive offerings
- Value is perceived by customers
- More customers buy more products

and decrease the threat of competition through competitive advantage protection. As depicted in **Exhibit 2.4,** effective innovation can serve both roles concurrently. In fact, the more innovation-oriented a company is, the faster it achieves both roles.

The purpose of a corporation should be more than merely to maximize shareholder wealth. In fact, very often this goal can cause a company to develop strategies that, over the long term, result in exactly

Exhibit 2.4

The Benefits of Innovation Effectiveness

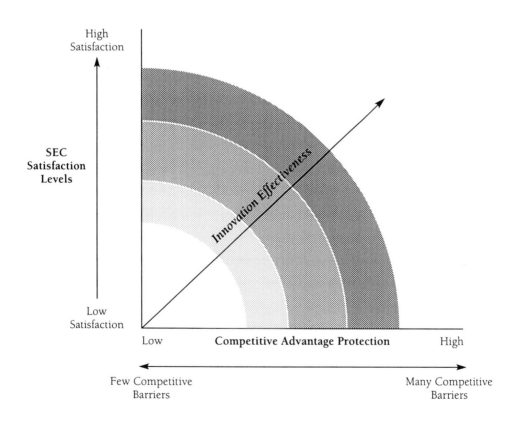

the reverse. Moreover, shareholders want more today than just quarterly earning gains. Many want companies to treat their employees better, become far more environmentally responsible, and invest in the long term rather than continually harvesting short-term yields. Shareholders are seeking values-based leaders, not hierarchical managers.

There are more employees in this country than there are shareholders, and more customers than either employees or shareholders. The three constituencies are totally interdependent.

Employees need customers to buy what they make or deliver; shareholders need employees to leverage their capital into goods and services that can be purchased; and customers are dependent on shareholders to invest funds needed to make products they want to buy. That's the self-regenerative power of innovation. Each needs to be satisfied, and innovation can satisfy all three. As depicted in **Exhibit 2.5**, customers buy products made by employees. This in turn generates profits, enables employee compensation to increase, and enhances shareholder wealth through higher stock prices and dividends. Innovation is the axle on which the profit wheel rotates. It provides the balance, power, and fuel to keep the wheel turning over time.

Exhibit 2.5

The Interdependency Wheel of SEC Satisfaction

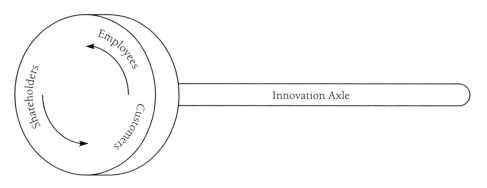

Gaining New Product Benefits

To think about innovation strategically also calls for looking at new products from the perspective of perceived benefits—that is, benefits of the product as perceived by consumers or end-users. Frequently, companies will view a new product as highly innovative because it leverages a proprietary technology or represents a totally new business for a company. However, this does not necessarily equate to a new set of benefits delivered to or perceived by the consumer.

As shown in **Exhibit 2.6**, the level of benefit newness should be determined relative to customer perceptions and competitive offerings, not according to its degree of newness to the company. Usually these

Exhibit 2.6

Perceptions of New Product Benefits

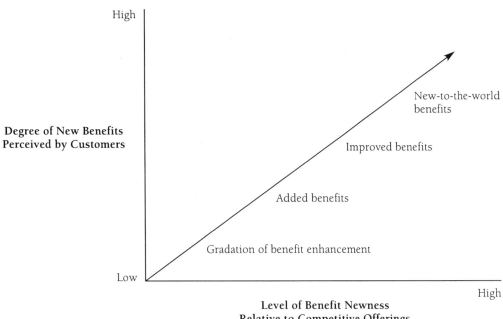

two dimensions correlate fairly closely to each other. If there are no competitive products that offer a similar benefit to consumers, it will usually be perceived as having a high degree of benefit newness. The level of perceived newness of product benefits increases as follows:

- Gradation of benefit enhancement in an existing product
- Added benefits in an existing product
- Improved benefits
- New-to-the-world benefits

Let's look at some examples of this. Thermoscan™ is a new type of thermometer that takes temperature readings from the ear. This infrared tympanic thermometer records the infrared heat generated by the eardrum and displays a person's temperature in less than two seconds.

Consumers perceive the benefits of the tympanic thermometer as very new. It's much easier to take a child's temperature, it's more hygienic, and the temperature readings are quicker and more accurate. When compared to the standard thermometer, this product provides multiple new benefits. Competitive advantage protection fuels the benefits advantage for a new product and makes it more difficult for competition to follow suit.

When the first fax machine was commercialized, it clearly enjoyed new-to-the-world benefits. Relative to its service competitors (i.e., UPS, Federal Express, and other overnight delivery services), this product offered the time-saving benefit of delivering a letter instantly. However, after the market was filled with fax machines, the only way to gain a competitive edge was by offering improved or added benefits. The plain paper fax achieved this. The new benefits to the end-user were no more messy thermal paper and ease in copying.

In contrast, look at the series of failures that companies experienced as they tried to partake in the "clear" craze. Clear soaps, clear gas, and clear colas. These all failed. Why? Because there was no new benefit of any meaning or significance to consumers. Marketing people might have thought that "clear" was a new benefit, but it "clearly" was not seen as such by consumers.

So, looking at the level of newness of an innovation can't be done within the vast corridors of a company. Benefits advantage must be determined by the consumer and according to *consumers'* perceptions of the degree of benefit enhancement. Benefit differentiation should be compared to other offerings and alternative, substitutable products currently on the market.

Obviously, the strategic positioning of innovations that embrace new-to-the-world or improved benefits have a longer period to enjoy high margins before competition follows.

An Innovation Blueprint

As described in my first book, *Managing New Products: The Power of Innovation,* most successful companies have both an innovation blueprint and an innovation strategy that describe the role of new products in achieving their overall growth objectives and strategy. The innovation blueprint should describe what a company wants new products to accomplish during the first three to five years. Does the company want new products to protect gross margins, defend against foreign competition, or utilize excess capacity? Additionally, the innovation blueprint describes the importance and purpose of new products relative to alternative growth modes (e.g., acquisitions, expansion of existing business share, strategic alliances).

Elements of the Blueprint

Do you have an innovation blueprint in place? If not, why not? How can you expect employees to be excited about or dedicated to innovation if they don't know management's perspective? Companies that have an innovation blueprint give employees greater confidence and comfort in knowing that what they're doing with innovation really does count. An innovation blueprint should include the following:

- A description of the overall growth role that new products will play in the company's growth strategy
- An estimated five-year budget that indicates the level of development expenditures and intended investment capital for the entire new products effort
- A profile of the human resource requirements
- A broad revenue target for the composite of all new products launched during the planned period, including either a total revenue number or percentage of sales
- A description of how the role of new products will mesh with other growth modes (e.g., acquisitions, licensing, strategic alliances, and contract arrangements)
- An articulation of top management's expectations for new products and its intended level of involvement (i.e., guidelines and performance benchmarks that define a successful new product development program and management's activities and type of participation in the process)

The worst type of innovation blueprint is a list of new product projects. If your company has such a list, burn the list at once if it is intended to serve as a proxy for an innovation blueprint. It is totally meaningless and distorts the objectives, focus, and level of commitment to new products. It accomplishes nothing more than generating a lot of aggravation. Many top executives proudly show off their lists of new product projects. They adopt a "my list is longer than yours" mentality. However, when the time comes to commit $1.5 million or $15 million to one new product launch, the enthusiasm suddenly dissipates.

Benefits of the Blueprint

The innovation blueprint is a concrete and tangible form of top-management commitment. It reinforces the need for top management to lay itself on the line concerning the future role of new products. It's a management "contract" that articulates support for long-term innovation. It also shakes out many skeletons from top management's closets, such as, "It looks like a great opportunity, but we just don't have the funds to support it this quarter—or next." Then why has some ambitious manager been working day and night to develop a prototype?

The innovation blueprint also enables the people working on new products to have some faith that all of their frustrations and anxieties are worth it. It promotes security, offers long-term perspective, and establishes a common set of expectations. More concretely, it is a written document that expresses the importance of new products to the company and the role new products will play in shaping the company's future.

The main advantage of a blueprint is that it requires senior management to give some thought to their expectations for new products. In addition, it begins to shape a commitment for the people and funding required to meet the innovation expectations.

Developing an Innovation Strategy

An innovation strategy consists of three key components:

1. New product or service financial goals and growth gap

2. Strategic roles that define the strategic mission of new products

3. Screening criteria that provide a series of filters through which to pass new product ideas

The innovation strategy sets up a road map for how the growth objectives of a company will be met through internally generated new products and services. Although the innovation blueprint sets up broad guidelines to steer innovation, the innovation strategy offers more specific details for guiding innovation efforts. In effect, it's the innovation planning document. It enables people to think about why they're planning to do innovation before they begin.

As you begin to craft an innovation strategy, take a look at your company's previous five-year new product performance. Start by identifying all new products or services that were commercialized during the past five years. Secure the relevant financial information for each new product, including annual revenues, gross profits, development costs, variance from original forecasts, and the like. Once the pertinent information for each new product has been collected, the results should be consolidated. Keep in mind the key purpose of this exercise, which is to determine how your overall new products portfolio has performed, not any single new product. The real value of this exercise lies in understanding the underlying reasons for why or how performance results were achieved or not achieved.

For example, a $350 million consumer durables manufacturer launched 15 new products during a five-year period. As its new product scorecard depicts in **Exhibit 2.7**, six of them met originally forecast sales projections and eight are still on the market. This translates to a 40 percent success rate and a 55 percent survival rate, respectively. Having invested $16.8 million in development costs to generate those 15 new products, the new product portfolio cumulatively returned $107.5 million in net operating earnings during a five-year period. This is an amazingly high return on an innovation investment. If the company had invested that same $16.8 million in the stock market, and if, on average, it yielded an annual return of 15 percent, the total investment would have grown only to $33.8 million, approximately $74 million less than the amount realized through the company's innovation efforts.

Exhibit 2.7

Consumer Durables Manufacturer's New Product Scorecard

- New products launched: 15

- Still on the market (survival rate): 8 (55%)

- Met original net sales projections (success rate): 6 (40%)

- Cumulative net sales generated (in thousands): $1,509,336

- New product net sales as a percentage of total category: 88.4%

- Cumulative gross profits generated (in thousands): $933,175

- New product gross profits as a percentage of total category: 84.3%

- Total development costs (in thousands): $16,819

- Cumulative NOE (net operating earnings) generated (in thousands): $107,498

  — $117,224 from Products A, B, C

  — $(9,726) from remaining 12 launches

Interestingly, three new products in particular had generated the bulk of the incremental earnings. Twelve of the new products either broke even, generated a slight profit, or lost money. But that's to be expected from any new products portfolio. What was management's perspective on their company's new products performance prior to showing them this new products scorecard? It was typical. They viewed their performance as poor, because they had had numerous new product failures. They realized that they had achieved a few winners, but they truly had no idea how well their innovation efforts, in total, had done.

You need to know where you've been before you can create a plan to define where you want to head. You also need to know how innovative your new product efforts have been. As shown in **Exhibit 2.8**, approximately 52 percent of total revenue generated in 1994 came from new-to-the-world products. This indicates the revenue and profit potential of investing in truly new and "radical" innovation. In fact, 42 percent of the cumulative new product profits over five years came from new-to-the-world products. This illustrates an important benefit of creating a successful innovation mindset: innovation *does* pay for itself.

Growth Gap

Now you're ready to develop the new products growth gap, or the revenues to be satisfied by new products during the next five years. You'll want to compare your desired revenue growth in five years to your planned revenues (based on historical and current product growth rates). The difference is the growth gap, which needs to be filled. You'll next need to determine how much of the gap should be satisfied by new products. As illustrated in **Exhibit 2.9**, for example, if a $360 million company's revenue goal is to grow 11 percent annually, its desired revenue performance will be to achieve $600 million by 1999. This translates to a new products revenue growth gap of approximately $273 million. If no new products are introduced during the next five years,

Exhibit 2.8

Historical New Product Net Sales by Product Type

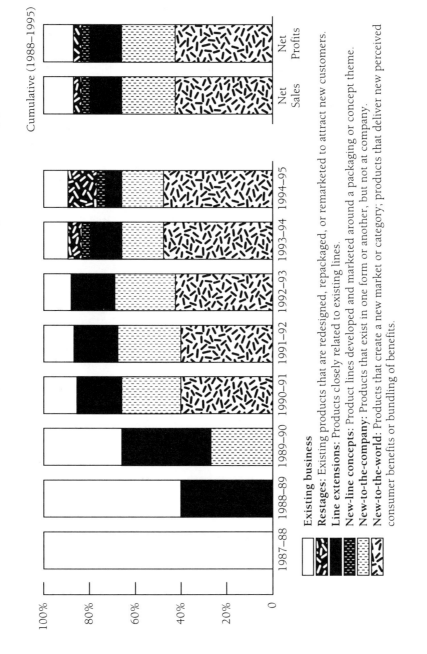

Existing business

Restages: Existing products that are redesigned, repackaged, or remarketed to attract new customers.

Line extensions: Products closely related to existing lines.

New-line concepts: Product lines developed and marketed around a packaging or concept theme.

New-to-the-company: Products that exist in one form or another, but not at company.

New-to-the-world: Products that create a new market or category; products that deliver new perceived consumer benefits or bundling of benefits.

Source: Kuczmarski & Associates, Inc., client interviews.

the existing business will gradually decline by 1.5 percent annually, to less than $334 million by 1999. Even though the business has grown 21 percent annually during the past five years, management recognizes that competition has intensified, category growth has slowed, their revenue base is larger, and international expansion has not panned out as desired.

The question is, "What is the appropriate investment in people and dollars to fill this growth gap?" You'll need to examine the complement of people and financial resources required to ensure this gap gets filled. The benefit of establishing a new products growth gap is that it puts a stake in the ground to calibrate new product expectations. It also serves to give management and new product participants a common understanding and an agreed-upon target for expected results of the company's innovation efforts.

Strategic Roles

To further link innovation to business strategy, you need to identify new product strategic roles. That is, beyond adding more revenues and profits, what strategic missions should new products serve to support the growth goals of the company?

Strategic roles help to identify the way in which new products can further build the existing business or take the company into new businesses and categories. In developing strategic roles, managers should ask: "What are the roles that new products should play in serving and supporting both the existing and the desired new businesses?" Each strategic role should be aimed at fulfilling a business requirement, whether to strengthen existing product lines or to provide a way to enter new businesses or markets. Both types of strategic roles are intended to further identify how new products can best serve the growth goals of the company. New product strategic roles can be classified into requisite and expansive roles:

Exhibit 2.9

The New Products Growth Gap

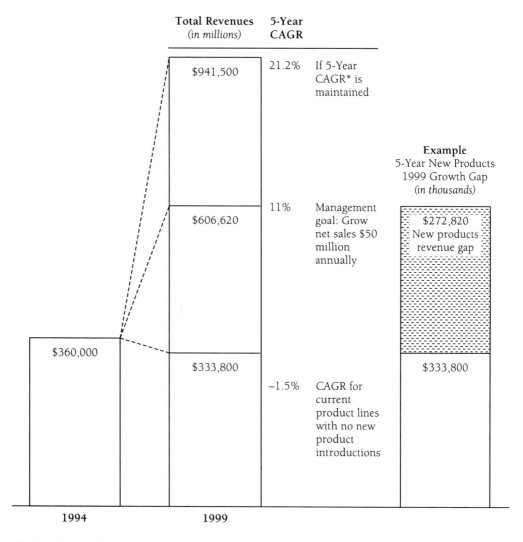

Total Revenues *(in millions)*	5-Year CAGR	
$941,500	21.2%	If 5-Year CAGR* is maintained
$606,620	11%	Management goal: Grow net sales $50 million annually
$333,800	−1.5%	CAGR for current product lines with no new product introductions

Example
5-Year New Products
1999 Growth Gap
(in thousands)

$272,820
New products
revenue gap

$333,800

$360,000

1994   1999

*CAGR = Compound annual growth rate.

- **Requisite roles:** Define the role new products are expected to satisfy in defending, expanding, bolstering, or increasing the competitive advantage of existing product lines.

- **Expansive roles:** Define ways that new products can get a company into new segments, categories, markets, benefit sets, or businesses.

An example of strategic roles to guide new products is illustrated in **Exhibit 2.10.** It is an example of how a $300 million water purification company set up a strategic role framework to guide its innovation efforts.

Exhibit 2.10

Strategic Roles

Five-Year Business Direction for Future New Product Development Efforts
Be the innovative market leader of water quality enhancement products meeting consumers' varied needs and wants to clean, purify, and satisfy taste requirements for the water they drink.

Requisite Roles:
Define ways new products can satisfy defending, expanding and bolstering the current business.

Expansive Roles:
Define ways new products can propel the business into new categories, markets, and segments.

A. Build market share through leadership in water purification innovation.

B. Address key consumer dissatisfaction areas via improved delivery systems and/or new forms.

C. Expand size of category by understanding and creating products that appeal to non-users.

D. Expand business by broadening the base of core benefits delivered to improve water quality in consumers' homes.

E. Expand usage by addressing the relationship between health and taste benefits.

There is often a high degree of overlap between requisite and expansive roles. What's important is that new product roles be developed to define what a company expects new products to do beyond increasing revenues and profits. No single role stands as a touchstone. Successful companies have used a variety of new product types to satisfy a wide range of roles. Often, a new-to-the-world or new-to-the-company product will satisfy expansive roles, whereas line extensions, repositionings, improvements, and cost reductions will be used to fulfill requisite roles. However, each new product type can potentially meet many roles.

Requisite Role Functions

Requisite roles are usually geared toward the following functions:

1. Defending or protecting a business from competition
2. Supporting or expanding the existing business
3. Applying an internal strength, such as a new technology or raw-material cost advantage, to strengthen the core competency of the business or product line

Requisite roles can be aimed at solving existing business problems, for example, utilizing excess capacity or waste by-products, off-setting seasonal fluctuations in sales, or improving manufacturing costs.

Expansive Role Functions

Expansive roles often include enabling a company to do the following:

1. Enter a new category, market, or business
2. Develop products that will attract a totally new customer base
3. Leverage technology in a new way to offer new benefits
4. Provide access to a foreign market

Some of the more common roles that innovation can play as a tool for long-term goal attainment can be seen in **Exhibit 2.11.** These were identified as the top strategic roles by companies surveyed in a study conducted by Kuczmarski & Associates in 1993. The study encompassed 11,000 new product launches during a five-year period.

What's interesting is that the strategic roles used differ greatly from one company to another. No one role is better than the other, because the appropriateness of each is totally dependent on a company's business strategy. However, more successful companies have "utilizing a new technology" as a strategic business role three times as often as do less-successful companies. In addition, successful companies are more likely to set up a new product strategic role aimed at "gaining or maintaining a competitive advantage" than are less-successful companies. This suggests that companies that innovate understand the power of innovation to build competitive advantage.

Typically, new product strategic roles provide consensus and a road map for defining the expectations for innovation. Knowing what these expectations are, at the outset, is essential for creating an innovation mindset. The reason for this is rather simple. People need to know what they are trying to achieve. They need the big picture, the long-term perspective, the end-point, the destination. Unless they know where the goal line is, they'll never be able to score. Strategic business roles for innovation provide the goal posts so that people know which direction to run. These roles provide a new products team with a perspective on what it is that new products must achieve for fueling the company's business strategy.

Screening Criteria

The final ingredient of the new products strategy is the establishment of screening criteria. These screens should be viewed as minimal thresholds that a new idea, concept, or developed prototype must pass through.

Exhibit 2.11

Strategic Roles of New Products in Successful Companies

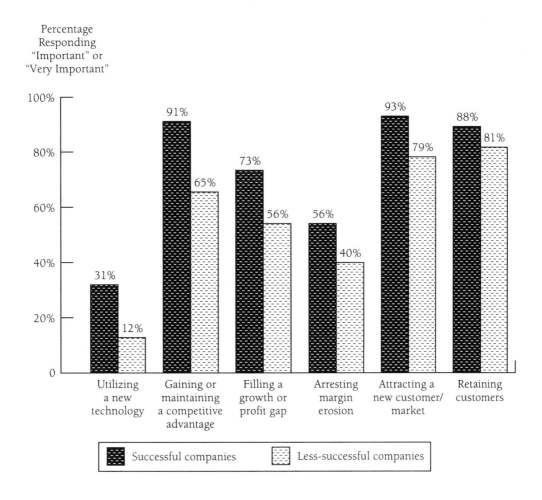

Percentage Responding "Important" or "Very Important"

Successful companies

Less-successful companies

Source: "Winning New Product and Service Practices for the 1990s," Kuczmarski & Associates, Inc., 1993.

The concept and tested product screens include financial hurdles. There are three points in the new product development process that warrant screens:

1. After idea generation, to prune down the list and select a few ideas for concept development
2. After business analysis, to determine which concepts should move to prototype development
3. After market testing, prior to commercialization or product launch

These three points are depicted in **Exhibit 2.12**, which highlights where screening should take place at certain stages of the development process.

Appendix 2A provides a set of questions for evaluating and screening new ideas, concepts, and tested products at the three appropriate stages of the process. Tied to the concept screens and tested product screens should be financial hurdles that you set by new product type. Remember, your financial expectations should be differentiated according to perceived level of risk, which varies by new product type.

In summary, innovation can be viewed as an integral component of a company's business strategy, as shown in **Exhibit 2.13**. Competitive advantage protection will help to enhance growth and profits and help to increase shareholder, employee, and customer satisfaction. An innovation blueprint and strategy can help to propel and activate a company's winning business strategy.

Exhibit 2.12

Screens Linked to New Product Development Process

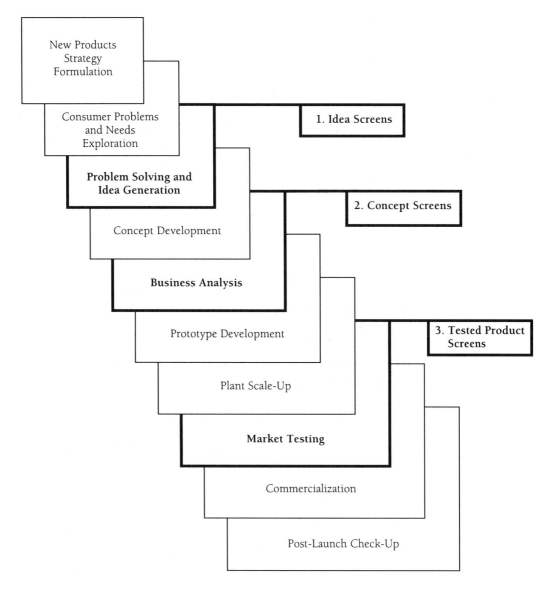

Exhibit 2.13

Innovation's Role in Business Strategy

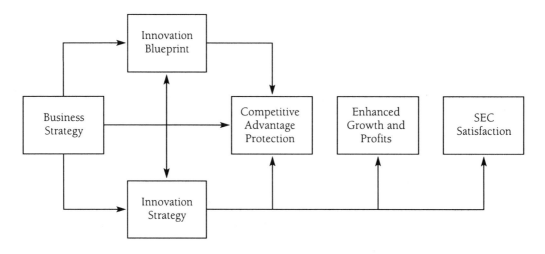

Innovation Checklist: Developing Competitive Advantage

1. Manage risk according to upside profit potential, not just potential downside cost savings.

2. Pursue higher innovation returns through higher-risk forms of innovation providing totally new benefits.

3. Assess benefit newness by customer perceptions, not just in relation to competitive offerings.

4. Develop shareholder satisfaction with long-term, values-based leadership in the marketplace.

5. Provide new products team with an innovation blueprint that goes far beyond a list of new product projects.

6. Create a five-year innovation strategy to specify targets for the new products portfolio as a whole.

Evaluation and Screening Questions

Screen One: Selecting High-Potential Ideas

Strategic Screens

Fit with strategic objectives

- Does the new product idea fit within the strategic roles?
- Does the idea have international potential?
- Is the idea consistent with the company's environmental posture?

Exploits internal strengths

- Is the idea manufacturable, either in-house or through an outside vendor?
- Does the idea capitalize on channel/sales strengths?
- Does the idea fit with company core technologies? If not, can the technology be developed internally, purchased, or licensed?

Source of competitive advantage

- Are competitors present in the potential segment?
- Does the idea capitalize on an existing trend or establish a new trend?

Consumer Screens

Need intensity

- Will the product have a broad or a narrow appeal?
- Does the idea satisfy the expressed need?

Uniqueness/ differentiation

- Does the idea satisfy an existing or unmet need?
- Does the idea deliver an important consumer benefit?

Financial Screens

Size of opportunity

- What is the universe of customers in the potential segment?

Impact on existing business

- Will the idea add significant incremental sales?
- What resources are required to continue development?

Return potential

- How big will sales revenues need to be for this potential product to break even?

(continued)

Evaluation and Screening Questions

Screen Two: Selecting High-Impact Concepts

Strategic Screens

Fit with strategic objectives

- Does the new product concept capitalize on or build on the existing brand?
- Can the concept potentially provide a competitive advantage?

Exploits internal strengths

- Does the concept utilize existing equipment and/or technology?
- Can the idea be distributed through existing channels?

Source of competitive advantage

- Is the concept patentable or is the technology proprietary?
- Can we achieve a sustainable or first-to-market advantage against current and potential competitors?
- Can we insulate ourselves from competition with respect to cost structures, process design, raw materials, or regulatory barriers?

Consumer Screens

Need intensity

- Does the concept deliver against an unmet need?
- What purchase intent scores did the concept achieve?

Uniqueness/ differentiation

- What uniqueness score did the concept achieve?
- Does the concept extend the benefits available to consumers?

Financial Screens

Size of opportunity

- What are revenues, margins, and profits expected to be?
- How much will the concept cost to manufacture?

Impact on existing business

- Will the concept cannibalize existing business?
- Is the concept expected to grow the category?

Return potential

- What discount rate should be applied to this concept?
- What is the expected net profit and return on investment for the concept?

(continued)

Evaluation and Screening Questions

Screen Three: Optimizing the New Product Offering

Strategic Screens

Fit with strategic objectives

- Does the product deliver against strategic objectives?

Exploits internal strengths

- Does the product capitalize on distribution strengths?

Source of competitive advantage

- Does the product satisfy the consumer need better than competitive offerings?

Consumer Screens

Need intensity

- Have in-home or field tests indicated consumer acceptance of the product?
- Have in-home or field tests indicated consumer preference for the product versus a relevant standard?

Uniqueness/ differentiation

- Is the product truly distinctive?
- Do the communication strategies position the product uniquely in consumers' minds?

Financial Screens

Size of opportunity

- Does the product offer significant opportunities for future line extensions?

Impact on existing business

- What are the implications of proceeding to market?

Return potential

- Does the product achieve manufacturing cost estimates and margin projections?
- Does it achieve profitability goals and return objectives?

chapter three

Is an Innovation Mindset Necessary?

Overcoming the Sisyphus Pattern

American companies need to learn the trick of combining large size (with the accompanying economics of scope and access to capital and markets) with agility and innovation. Foster smaller units with an entrepreneurial spirit, that can join teams together, without a top-heavy bureaucracy above them, to make global decisions.

—Rosabeth Moss Kanter

Maybe an innovation mindset isn't needed for successful innovation to occur. And maybe the earth will be invaded by Martians who will take over the planet. Well, it certainly is possible, but at least for the time being it's highly unlikely. The only way to assure that successful innovation will happen is to adopt an innovation mindset. This chapter defines and examines the value of developing an innovation mindset. It will prove that it is well worth your time and energy to do so.

The CEO Factor

For nearly two decades, I have frequently been asked, "What can I do if the CEO and senior management group do not appear to be truly committed to new products?" After years of trying to address this question, I've finally learned the answer: "Get out of new products or leave the company. Don't bother one day longer to fight this uphill battle." Without top management support for and belief in innovation, you'll end up like Sisyphus, the King of Corinth, who was doomed to continuously push a boulder up to the top of a steep hill, only to watch it roll back down again.

If the company succession plan has identified you as the next CEO, then hang in there. If that's not the case, and the current and future CEOs lack an innovation mindset, then just hang it up. You can't win—move into manufacturing, sales, marketing, or finance. Find a new company with an innovation mindset.

Simply put, CEOs drive innovation. There's no other designated driver. Even with CEOs who create an innovation mindset within their companies, failures happen. But recognizing and accepting failure as an intrinsic and inherent part of innovation initiates the right mindset.

So what can be done? If innovation and new products or services are a core ingredient of your company's business strategy, then take a deep breath and plunge into the innovation pool. Don't expect to delegate this down, over, or up. It won't work. As a top manager, "every breath you take, every move you make, every step you take" is watched, analyzed, and interpreted by your employees. This suggests the need for you to breathe, speak, and walk innovation. It's the only effective way to build an innovation mindset.

If innovation is not important to your company's strategy, that's fine; just let employees know that. Avoid exploiting some young, aspiring manager who wants to develop the next new-to-the-world product and believes he or she will be rewarded for its success. Be honest with your organization. Put a stake in the ground and let employees see where you place it on the innovation playing field.

The CEO factor is the most important variable in the innovation equation. Without CEO involvement and belief in innovation, it won't be successful.

The Innovation Headache Cure

Trying to make innovation happen, being successful, and being profitable can be a major headache. Think of an innovation mindset as aspirin, which relieves tension, relaxes muscles, and enables people to concentrate. You might be able to develop successful new products and services in spurts, but an innovation mindset provides a solid foundation—stamina—for continuous innovation to occur over a long period.

In short, an innovation mindset can provide three overriding benefits to an organization:

- Increased understanding of how innovation can become an integral part of business strategy achievement
- Elevated awareness of the importance of innovation and a desire to keep it top-of-mind
- Greater credibility in and recognition of innovation as a way of professional life

Some of the benefits of an innovation mindset are subtle, yet critical. (See **Exhibit 3.1.**) The top ten benefits of an innovation mindset help to explain why it's worth your time and effort to develop one within your company.

There are two additional aspects of innovation that are important to keep in mind. First, it takes time. It can't be cranked out in a two-week or even a two-month time frame. Innovation requires a gestation period. It is not a linear process, it is iterative. It requires inductive instead of deductive reasoning. It needs room to breathe, grow, and develop. So be patient and accept the time-sensitive nature of innovation.

Exhibit 3.1

Top Ten Benefits of Instilling an Innovation Mindset

1. An expanded, futuristic vision of the business, including the strategic roles that innovation can satisfy

2. Motivated team members who are rewarded financially, commensurate with the market performance of the new products they launch

3. Effective measurement indices enabling the company to determine its return from innovation investments and calibrate future expenditure levels, depending on strategic roles

4. Improved up-front consumer research, which explores the problems and unmet needs in a defined category to help guide idea generation

5. An alignment of technology and R&D resources against new product strategic roles to increase both efficiency and effectiveness

6. Committed and supportive functional and senior managers to ensure the "right" people resources and funds are dedicated to innovation

7. A pervasive and optimistic attitude about innovation that is felt and endorsed by all employees

8. A systematic development process that enables new product participants to know their roles at each step of the process and to understand their accountability and decision-making criteria

9. Acceptance of business judgment, intuition, experience, and insight as additional "tools" to use in the development process

10. Values that encourage and foster a belief in innovation as a legitimate and leverageable "intangible asset" for accelerating stock price and increasing future earnings

Second, it's a fragile process, like most creative endeavors. You can't tell an artist to paint a canvas that will generate a $100,000 price tag. Similarly, you can't just tell a new products team that you want them to create a specific $10 million new product within the next 90 days. (Although I've heard senior executives do exactly that.) You should encourage, support, trust, and nurture the teams that are undertaking innovation.

So creating an innovation mindset can cure many of the headaches, ailments, and sores that often arise during initial attempts at innovation. Creating an innovation mindset is an investment, but it's well worth the cost.

Avoid the Killer Mindset—Adopt an Awakener Mindset

Killer instincts might be just fine, but killer mindsets are bad. A killer mindset is one that is usually looking for excuses to kill a new product idea or concept. In contrast, an awakener mindset is one that is always looking for a way to breathe new life into a concept. Look at it differently; re-energize some of its benefits; develop a new positioning angle to bring it to life again. An awakener mindset searches for ways to improve and enhance a concept. This type of person takes a sleepy idea, awakens it, and turns it into a giant of a new product.

An awakener mindset also enables consumers to share a big part of the awakening. An awakened new product is one that has had an alarm go off from the perspective of solving a consumer problem or addressing an intense consumer need.

The most demoralizing wet blanket that can be thrown over the shoulders of a new products team often comes from the CEO. Try putting these "blankets" in the dryer before using them—in fact, avoid them at all cost. Innovation mindsets can happen in small, incremental ways. They evolve gradually. You can't fix everything overnight, but you can reverse the myth of Sisyphus and push up smaller boulders that do stay at the top of the mountain.

Combining Efficiency and Effectiveness

Successful creators of innovation mindsets combine efficiency with effectiveness. They understand the dual objectives that drive profitable innovation: (1) increased speed to market (efficiency) and (2) higher success rates of new products launched (effectiveness). There is often a conflict and series of trade-offs that occur in trying to achieve these two objectives. Increasing the speed can negatively impact the chances of launching a quality, successful new product. In turn, taking too much time trying to develop only "winners" is likely to cause time delays in launching products to market. This might allow your competition to beat you to the draw. The ideal is to keep both objectives in balance and work toward achieving both simultaneously.

Recently, it seems as if most companies have focused their attention on the speed-to-market objective. Parallel processing, concurrent engineering, and simulated test marketing are all good approaches, and they will save time. However, when management develops a schedule-driven or launch-date mindset, it can be too often misinterpreted by new product teams. Often, I'll hear shouted out from the corner office of a company, "Do whatever it takes to meet the launch date!" This is a frequent mandate of top management.

Speed can kill new products. It can result in time-pressured managers skipping steps, inadequate testing, and insufficient creative thinking to shape a concept fully. The worst thing overemphasizing speed can do, though, is demoralize a new products team. Again, new product innovators are involved in a creative process, which has a certain time dimension in and of itself. Time guidelines should be set, but when speed to market becomes the paramount objective, it can dilute the creative and analytic processes that generate solutions (i.e., new products) to consumers' problems (i.e., needs and wants).

So company leaders should establish a mindset that reinforces the mutual importance of both of these goals. Bringing new product failures to market more quickly is not the result you desire. Successful leaders take responsibility for the seven initiatives shown in **Exhibit 3.2**, which enable a company to focus on increasing the success rates of new products launched while providing for their development in a timely manner.

Exhibit 3.2

The Seven Initiatives of Innovation Mind-Setters

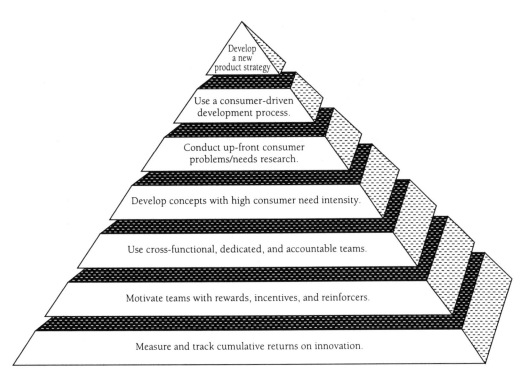

Develop a new product strategy

Use a consumer-driven development process.

Conduct up-front consumer problems/needs research.

Develop concepts with high consumer need intensity.

Use cross-functional, dedicated, and accountable teams.

Motivate teams with rewards, incentives, and reinforcers.

Measure and track cumulative returns on innovation.

Innovation Requires a Holistic Approach

If we were to examine the mental makeup of successful innovators, we might find seven functions that all work together. Too often, senior managers will decide to take the innovation bull by the horns and aggressively pursue a new process technique, try out a new team-building approach, or create a new incentive system. Alone, any one of these will not foster innovation. But this should not come as a surprise. Successful innovation requires a holistic approach. You can't eliminate one lobe of the brain and expect it to function. Likewise, you can't overlook one of the core components of instilling an innovation mindset and expect new products to emerge.

All parts of the brain are connected and share an electrical charge. The same is true for an innovation mindset. The seven essential "lobes" of an innovation mindset are depicted in **Exhibit 3.3:**

- **Innovation Blueprint:** A vision that defines the future role that innovation should play relative to the long-term goals of the company. Expected overall investments and returns should be included.

- **Innovation Strategy:** A framework that bridges the business strategy and the new product goals and resources. An innovation strategy has three key functions:

  1. It defines the financial goals and growth gap for new products and the revenue/profit gaps to be filled by them.

  2. It outlines strategic roles that new products are intended to satisfy in defending, protecting, or growing the existing business or in allowing the company to diversify into new markets, customer segments, or business categories.

  3. It requires that screening criteria are used to evaluate new product concepts and potential candidates for commercialization.

Exhibit 3.3

An Innovation Mindset

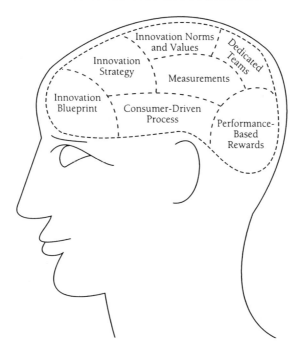

- **Consumer-Driven Process:** A step-wise development process that is systematic but flexible. The process begins with the identification of potential problem categories and consumer problems/needs and ends with market testing and commercialization.

- **Dedicated Teams:** The formation of cross-functional teams with motivated members. At a minimum, the team leader should be dedicated full time to the team with no other operating responsibilities other than innovation.

- **Performance-Based Rewards:** Psychic rewards including peer recognition, descriptive praise, exposure to top management, and "achievement" awards. In addition, use compensation approaches that reward new product performance and simulate an entrepreneurial experience by providing a mechanism for participants to invest in new products being developed.

- **Innovation Norms and Values:** Innovation values or beliefs and innovation norms, which set up the communications approaches and behavioral guidelines for the teams and other functional participants to work by.

- **Measurements:** Metrics that identify the return on innovation and investment requirements and innovation indices that track and monitor progress.

It is essential to recognize that each of these "lobes" must be in place to create an innovation mindset. Achieving two or three out of the seven is not enough. All have to be in place and reinforce each other. They should link together in a way that enables all employees to understand and share in the importance of innovation to the company.

Why doesn't an innovation mindset appear more frequently in companies? The primary fault lies with the ever-present bureaucratic mindset that pervades most corporations. It precludes the opportunity for an innovation mindset to grow.

Do You Have an Innovation Mindset?

Maybe you already have an innovation mindset. To find out, take the CEO Innovation Mindset test. Answer each of the questions in **Exhibit 3.4** and score five points for each answer in the affirmative. Be brutally honest with yourself.

Many senior managers score relatively low on this test. For some, innovation is merely a list of new product projects with associated financial forecasts for each. When innovation is nothing more than a

Exhibit 3.4

The CEO Innovation Mindset Test

Answer yes or no to each question.

1. Do I currently incorporate innovation into our business plan as a strategic lever for increasing satisfaction with shareholders, employees, and customers? _____

2. Have I consciously used innovation and launched new products to help accelerate my company's stock price or increase my company's value? _____

3. Have I purposely developed a balanced portfolio of new product types with varying degrees of risk ranging from radically new-to-the-world to line extensions and repositionings? _____

4. Do I teach my management team to view innovation as an investment opportunity rather than as a cost center that negatively impacts quarterly earnings? _____

5. Do I have a commonly agreed-upon innovation strategy in place that links the role of innovation and new products to our business strategy? _____

6. Have I made innovation an attractive career path for employees to pursue? _____

7. Do I regularly celebrate new product failures with as much fervor as new product successes with all team members? _____

8. Do I uniformly communicate and act in ways that clearly convey trust in the cross-functional teams that are activating innovation? _____

9. Do I stimulate an entrepreneurial environment by having a performance-based compensation system in place for new product participants? _____

10. Do I measure and communicate throughout the organization the return on innovation for our company? _____

(continued)

Exhibit 3.4 (continued)

The CEO Innovation Mindset Test

11. Do I really know how much innovation costs, and do I set realistic return expectations for innovation? _____

12. Do I provide "ceilingless" and motivating compensation rewards to new product participants and allow them to invest in the new products they are developing? _____

13. Do I select the best people within the company (i.e., those I feel I can't afford to remove from the existing business) to activate the new products process? _____

14. Do I make sure we conduct consumer research prior to idea generation to identify problems and needs? _____

15. Do I ensure that idea generation is a problem-solving endeavor aimed at generating potential solutions to address consumer needs? _____

16. Do I maintain funding and resource allocation for innovation at a consistent level rather than pulling the plug after a "down" quarter? _____

17. Do I truly accept that 40–50 percent of our future new product launches will fail? _____

18. Do all R&D people get at least 15 percent "free time" (unassigned to any specific project) to give them room to breathe and freedom to explore their own ideas? _____

19. Do I have a well-articulated technology strategy that defines technology platforms and areas of needed technical expertise to help support the innovation initiatives? _____

20. Do I hear others throughout the organization talk about my positive, enthusiastic, supportive, and "can-do" attitude toward innovation? _____

Scoring:

Give yourself five points for each yes answer and add up your score.

80+ **Outstanding:** You already have a strong innovation mindset.

60+ **Good:** You are evolving toward an innovation mindset.

<60 **Poor:** You have a negative mindset toward innovation.

project list with timelines and forecasts, it moves into an activity category. The mindset that emerges is one that focuses on time. How do we make the launch-date deadline? How do we increase the efficiency of performing the activities required to get new products to the market faster? How can we take less time to do more projects?

Less time and more speed are not the right measures for successful innovation. New products portfolio success rates and returns on innovation investment are. Getting many new product failures to market quickly will not generate profitable long-term returns.

Innovation, therefore, is not a list of new product projects. Rather, it is a mindset that believes in and values the role that innovation can play in accelerating stock price, supporting the business strategy, and increasing satisfaction to shareholders and employees. Higher returns and more satisfied customers will result in products that satisfy their needs or solve their problems.

Innovation Is Being Strangled

We are still being led in this country by top managers who tend to have a short-term business perspective. In their defense, we also still have a stock market that reacts severely to short-term earnings forecasts and reports. However, I strongly believe that both will change relatively soon, possibly within the next decade.

There are already several companies that are rewarded by shareholders for long-term, sustainable value creation, even amidst some short-term earnings downturns. Motorola and General Electric, for instance, are two companies that have instilled an innovation and entrepreneurial mindset into their companies. Although they are both massive, multibillion-dollar corporations, they have been able to weave innovation into their business strategies and use it as a core growth driver. According to Rosabeth Moss Kanter in a *Harvard Business Review* editorial (May–June 1992):

Bureaucracy has been the most highly evolved form of organization, responsible for industrial progress. It was rational.
It was efficient. It was also passionless. Bureaucracy was
designed for repetition, not innovation; for control, not
creativity.

She captures the essence of what I believe to be the major barrier
to innovation success—the corporate mindset. Don't blame a lack of
innovation on the Japanese, global competition, or the stock market.
Blame yourselves. I have yet to see a product line or business that can't
be expanded and competitively differentiated through innovation. But
only when innovation is managed correctly and only when a mindset
is inculcated in the hearts, minds, and souls of most employees can this
occur.

The future of U.S. corporations will depend greatly on their ability
to loosen the stranglehold currently binding innovation. Companies
need to unleash innovation. They must understand that new products
and services are the tools for building long-term growth. To do this, the
short-term earnings noose must come off. Take a risk, stand up to the
financial community, and shout loudly, "This company will be making
long-term investments for its future by focusing on and investing in
competitive advantage protection. These long-term growth strategies
might result in some short-term earnings decreases. Rest assured that
these investments in innovation will be aimed at maximizing shareholder returns."

You must not wait until innovation is in a crisis state, although
we might already be at that point. You should make a concerted effort
to change the return expectations from innovation investments. You
need to deepen your commitment to R&D spending, innovation expenditures, problem exploratory research, and the costs associated with
new product development.

It's time to tell the financial community that results will not be
measured in 90-day increments. Results that sustain take time. It's time
to loosen the stifling bureaucratic rules and procedures to open up a
new way of thinking—innovatively.

Total Innovation Involvement

An innovation mindset calls for all employees involved in innovation to be "believers." It's as simple as that. A belief that with the right innovation and technology strategy outlined, a new product development process in place, and adequate financial and human resources available, innovation will happen. Successful new products and services will result.

However, mindsets are not created overnight. They need time to evolve. That's one key reason why companies should continuously perform innovation. Fits and starts will stifle the entire innovation process. Turning off the innovation valve can be deadly. Once you turn the valve back on, it usually takes a minimum of three years before any new products will begin to flow again.

Four sets of players within a company are needed to develop and nurture an innovation mindset:

- **Innovation leaders,** who guide new product teams and endeavors
- **Senior managers,** who instill a positive, proactive, and supportive attitude to motivate innovation leaders
- **New products team participants,** who convey optimism, self-confidence, and a passion for innovation
- **Functional leaders,** who believe in the importance of new products and assign dedicated new products team members

This total innovation involvement must be activated by all four of these constituents equally and simultaneously. All four groups work hand in hand to provide the needed resources, motivation, and support. Consequently, all four groups need to communicate frequently. Forums should be established where regular exchange of information and ideas takes place among them. You can't just set up an innovation strategy, process, and teams and expect to operate on automatic pilot. It must be continuously pumped up and reactivated. Keeping up a balanced involvement of each constituency is tantamount to innovation success. (See **Exhibit 3.5.**)

Exhibit 3.5

Total Innovation Involvement

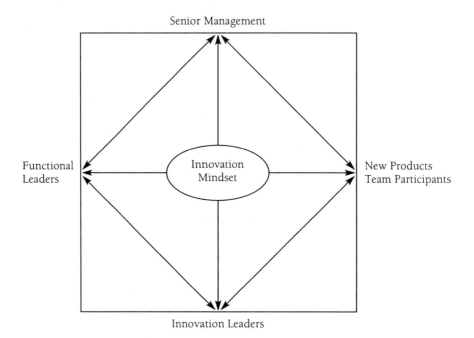

Using Disciplined Freedom

You need to give new products teams latitude to make mistakes and learn from them. You need to trust them. There should be a delicate balance maintained between rigor and flexibility, creativity and analysis, teamwork and individual achievement, and discipline and freedom.

Disciplined freedom provides team members with a sense of autonomy and entrepreneurialism, while giving them adequate direction and operating guidelines to help steer them through the uncertain path of innovation. It suggests that new products team members can think for themselves and use intuition, previous experience, and business judgment in decision making. It purports an environment that respects the views, opinions, and ideas of each team member. Collectively, it fosters a vibrant and energized team that is motivated to innovate.

Active listening and association-making are two skills that should be resident in new products team members. Listening intently to consumers is key. Piecing together bits of market or competitive information, consumer inputs, and functional data should help a new products team to assemble a puzzle, which eventually reveals a new product.

Delegating responsibility and full accountability to new products team members creates more individual commitment and buy-in to participate in innovation. As long as a sense of freedom is felt, new products participants are more likely to stand up for and develop an almost emotional attachment to a new product concept. You and your new products colleagues should convey emotion, enthusiasm, and passion. This is positive and should be encouraged daily.

Too often, enthusiasm is judged as frivolous emotion, which is a proxy for irrational thinking. Not true. Passion is a critical ingredient for sparking innovation. This passion or emotional freedom is harnessed by having in place an innovation strategy, process, screening criteria, and financial goals. The innovation road map should be defined, but there must be some flexibility for the drivers to take a variety of routes to reach their destinations.

Many CEOs focus on creating a sense of urgency for new products. They think that the right way to achieve this is to establish deadlines. Similar to a "stretch" goal, the well-intended CEO thinks that forcing a team to meet an unrealistic launch date will serve as a catalyst to motivate them.

All this technique does is demoralize the team and weaken the process, usually resulting in new product failures. Doing the right amount of up-front homework, spending more time on consumer testing, and conducting sound business analysis for a new concept will yield far better results than eliminating steps to save time and hasten the launch date. Granted, time to market is important. But there has to be a balance between doing the right things and doing things right. In the long run, spending adequate time on each stage in the development process saves time rather than wasting it. Disciplined freedom is a key part of an innovation mindset.

Disciplined freedom provides parameters that enable employees to feel comfortable working on innovation without fear of risking their careers. Companies that encourage the innovation mindset encourage people to be mavericks, be contrarian, and express emotion—almost to the point of obsession. Managers and employees involved with innovation need a sense of autonomy and the freedom to take risks.

The Characteristics of an Innovation-Minded CEO

Beyond establishing the right pieces of the innovation puzzle, top management must be active and visibly involved in innovation. Visibility is essential. You need to walk the corporate corridors, visit the R&D labs, attend some focus groups, and listen more and talk less to new products managers. Being visible means attending some new products team meetings, traveling on the same airplane (in coach) with other new products team members, or visiting a manufacturing plant that's making a new product.

You must also be willing to put your own career on the line. Take a stand. Make a commitment. Announce to the financial community, shareholders, and employees your role in, expectations for, and level of resource commitment being made to innovation. You have to shout it out again and again. You can scratch the press releases. You need to state it verbally yourself. You need to be held accountable for innovation results. Your paycheck should reflect overall success or failure in setting a results-oriented innovation mindset.

The following characteristic may be the most challenging for senior managers. You need to be humble. Passion is fine; ego isn't. Ego gets in the way of innovation. It serves no purpose. It taints one's perspective, because inherent to ego is the perception that one has all the answers. If we knew it all, we wouldn't need innovation. Ego can also diminish the spirit of a new products team. It tends to cast a shadow on the good thoughts and creative ideas of other individuals. Being humble recognizes that innovation is a fragile process requiring heavy doses of creativity.

Finally, adopt a willingness to interview potential new hires that would work in the new products area. Hiring the right type of people to manage innovation is at least as important as hiring a VP of manufacturing or VP of marketing. You can bet that the CEO will meet those two candidates if they are hired externally. The same should hold true for the innovation new hires.

When Do New Products Fail?

New products fail when consumers don't want to buy them. As trite as that may sound, managers who become consumed with their own new product favorites, without first determining the extent to which each has a high need-intensity or solves a consumer problem will usually fail.

This is why exploratory research and problem identification with a broad range of consumers should be the first step in the development process. New products people must become problem solvers, rather than just idea generators. Of course, creativity is a key component of solving problems, but the creative thinking should be focused against a problem.

In the 1993 "Winning Practices" study that our firm conducted, the number-one reason for new product failures was the lack of understanding of market needs. (See **Exhibit 3.6**.) Apparently, companies are still not listening to consumers well enough.

Exhibit 3.6

Reasons for New Product Failures

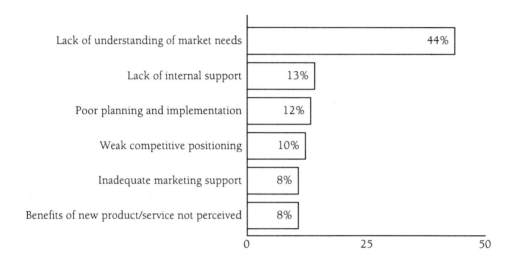

Source: "Winning New Product and Service Practices for the 1990s," Kuczmarski & Associates, Inc., 1993.

With the advent of highly sophisticated research techniques, how is this possible? In part, it's because many corporations are scared to take risks. They wait for a test to come back with quantitative scores on each new concept. They wait to read the normative research analysis that ranks concepts by the "top-two" boxes. They misinterpret the results. They don't use research as a tool to assist decision making, but rather as a club with which to bludgeon others. The research gives them "career protection." New products people have become reluctant to think about and judge new concepts on their own. They use market research test scores as a crutch and soon become unable to walk on their own. So there is still a dire need for better research on consumer problems that serves as the conduit to the new products pipeline.

The Future of Innovation

Innovation is becoming and will continue to build steam as the core component of a company's business strategy in the 21st century. The success formula for the future will look like **Exhibit 3.7.** Continued focus on lowering costs will be only one ingredient in future business success. Top managers will also need to change their leadership approaches and pay more attention to their most valuable asset, people. Effective innovation management will make or break companies in the future.

The days of reengineering costs out of the system and acquiring your way to financial prosperity are over. The hard work begins. Innovation is the new business frontier, and the successful executives will be the pioneers. You can't avoid it or skirt the issue—innovation is here to stay. Accept it and start creating an innovation mindset.

Exhibit 3.7

The Emerging Formula for Successful Innovation

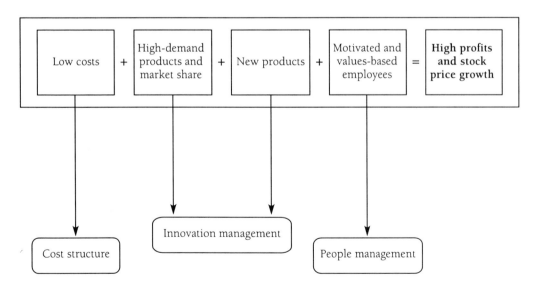

In concert with this evolutionary shift toward innovation, top executives will begin to endorse the following six innovation mindset tenets:

1. Innovation will be linked to and integrated with business strategy.
2. Innovation will become a separate function or department within a company.
3. Shareholders will appreciate and reward innovation more, and stock prices will reflect a company's effectiveness in innovation.
4. Companies will measure returns on innovation as the level of investment and performance expectations increase.
5. Team structures that reinforce an innovation mindset will be kept in place for long periods, and innovation will have its own career path.
6. New compensation mechanisms will be developed to reinforce a more entrepreneurial and risk-sharing environment.

Although some companies already recognize the truth of these issues, most are still in the dark ages. Many think that process enhancements will increase new products success. Process is important, but it is only one small part of the innovation success formula. To be effective at innovation, a company needs a development process, but having one in no way guarantees success. It's the holistic approach to innovation that will work.

Keep Your Eye on the Innovation Ball

In a *Wall Street Journal* op-ed, "The Graceful Exit of Ford's Chief," Paul Ingrassia writes about Donald Petersen, the former chairman of Ford Motor Company. He writes that Petersen adhered to three management principles:

- Focus on products instead of profits, and the latter will naturally follow.
- Give your people a say in running the show and a share in the rewards as well.
- Be consistent.

These three guiding principles are applicable to creating an innovation mindset. As Petersen stated, "Managing only for profits is like playing tennis with your eye on the scoreboard, and not on the ball." CEOs can't play the innovation game by just focusing on the financial results. They need to pick up the racket, hit the ball, and play a good game, drawing on their previous experience and innovative techniques.

Top managers need to practice innovation and let people know it. Playing the innovation game with consistency, getting up to bat frequently, hitting the ball passionately, and playing conscientiously will generate high scores. CEOs and new products players need to take personal responsibility for achieving high need-intensity innovations. It's the personal level of commitment that often gets shattered in non-innovative cultures.

Innovation: The New Corporate Conscience

Andrew Parsons, director of McKinsey & Company's New York office, writes in *Journal of Services Marketing* (Fall 1991):

> Innovative companies focus on customer value rather than technological advance or clever marketing. They innovate across all their functions and innovate up and down the business system with their suppliers and distributors. They have higher output—they do more, faster, and more often. Like great baseball players, they have records based on consistency and longevity as much as on genius.

Parsons presents three important messages that are essential for creating an innovation mindset:

1. Innovation must be driven by end-users.
2. Innovation is a way of thinking that should transcend all dimensions of a business.
3. Quantity and consistency counts.

Appropriately, an innovation mindset covers advertising and communications innovations, distribution innovations, trade management innovations, finance innovations, HR management innovations, manufacturing innovations, suppliers' relationships, strategic alliance innovations, technology innovations, and, oh yes, product and service innovations.

Consequently, top managers should create a new consciousness within their companies that makes everyone uneasy if effective innovation is not occurring. Call it a new corporate conscience, an advanced state of organizational self-awareness. It is the recognition that innovation must become an integral part of your daily thinking and daily business life. An innovation mindset is necessary. Our future U.S. competitiveness depends on it. Your own company survival depends on it.

Innovation Checklist: The Merck Formula

Former Merck, Inc. CEO Roy Vagelos established the following rules for instilling an innovation mindset:
1. Maintain a collegial atmosphere.
2. Allow assignment flexibility.
3. Tolerate failure.
4. Provide freedom to work on "personal" projects.
5. Decrease administrative distractions.

chapter four

Innovation and Rising Stock Values

Shareholders in the Driver's Seat

The notion that the market values only short-term earnings and ignores long-term value is a myth. Studies show the exact opposite. In the vast majority of cases, stock prices rise when companies report an increase in research and development spending. One study of 634 corporate announcements of strategic significance—new research projects, major capital expenditures, joint ventures, or product development initiatives—showed a strong positive response by the stock market.

—Michael Jacobs, *Break the Wall Street Rule*

Innovation potential will become a new watchword for the financial community. Shareholders in the future will want to identify and reward prodigiously those companies that are successful at managing ongoing innovation. Shareholders will indeed cause a rapid acceleration in innovation among U.S. corporations. They will demand innovation, and if they don't get it, they'll simply invest elsewhere.

Shareholders, the financial community, and even the government will dramatically increase their attention to innovation. This means that top executives must shift their focus as well. The rapid and inevitable acceleration of innovation among U.S. corporations is on its way.

The New Shareholder Mindset

Shareholders will want additional information for making investment decisions. They will be seeking more data that can be used to forecast a company's competitive strength. They will be less reliant on past company performance as a predictor of the future. They will become more interested in a company's future potential for successful innovation. Certainly, they'll want to see a company's past returns on innovation.

Shareholders will want to understand a company's vision, be acquainted with the long-term strategic plan, and more stringently assess the leadership qualifications, experience base, and commitment of the management team. They will want to have some concrete evidence that competitive advantage protection is under way. Why? Because shareholders are getting tired of the broken promises and "trust me" approach. Shareholders deserve to be treated as the owners of a corporation, because, in fact, they are. They've earned the right to understand the role that innovation will play, and how management plans to achieve it. The glossy annual reports won't cut it anymore. The staged, well-rehearsed "dog and pony" shareholder meetings will no longer receive applause. Shareholders will become far more judgmental about the value a CEO, in particular, brings to the innovation game.

Likewise, boards of directors will be more discriminating in evaluating the progress their companies are making toward innovation effectiveness. Evaluating the potential for innovation will become a primary measure that the financial community will want to track. They'll want to know how a company's innovation capabilities and core competencies will stack up to competition.

Shareholder Investment Criteria

What criteria will shareholders use ten years from now to select one stock over another? In the future, will shareholders use different variables to judge a company's stock attractiveness? Yes, they will, and innovation will influence their stock purchase decision-making process. Innovation effectiveness will be viewed as an excellent indicator of a company's future earnings stream.

Stock price appreciation and dividends will still count—big time. But shareholders in the future will look more intently at three revealing factors in assessing a stock's attractiveness. These include the following factors:

1. The caliber and leadership strength of the CEO and senior management team

2. The degree of competitive strength and long-range plan growth aggressiveness

3. The potential for competitive innovation and a high ROI (return on *innovation,* not return on investment)

Although these three factors may appear, at first, to be a bit "soft," they will become "hard" predictors for a shareholder to better judge a company's future performance.

Stock price reflects the market's perception of anticipated, future earnings performance of a company. A company's stock price is analogous to a wide-angled snapshot. It captures the past, present, and future all in one picture. It's a remarkably all-encompassing point-in-time measurement, which depicts where a company has been and where its shareholders expect it to head. Obviously, stock prices fluctuate from one day to the next, but over time they do reflect the future performance expectations of a company. Investors will want to better evaluate the competitive advantage protection potential of a company in order to estimate future performance. A successful innovation platform within a company can churn out future earnings.

The Effect on Senior Management

How will all of this impact top managers in the 21st century? You will not have to debate about whether or not to invest in innovation. The only question will be how much to invest and when. The "if" question goes away. The "how" question becomes paramount. Stock price will more accurately reflect a company's potential for future successful innovation.

This is a very important point, which sophisticated investors, visionary CEOs, and insightful stock analysts will begin to endorse and adopt. The basic approach for determining stock attractiveness in the future will include innovation potential. An innovation mindset will be acknowledged as the precursor for creating a stable of new products that will greatly contribute to future earnings. In effect, shareholders will be more focused on the major power source for future earnings—the innovation engine.

Granted, there will continue to be a multitude of variables that will impact stock price, but innovation effectiveness will attain unprecedented importance in valuing stock prices. Consequently, CEOs and senior managers should have their compensation schemes tied more directly to the tangible results of innovation. Of course, the more typical linkage of stock price appreciation to senior management bonuses and stock options will still be appropriate.

In many cases today, the gap between top management compensation and innovation effectiveness is widening. Pay-for-performance should become a more widely accepted compensation method. However, many executives don't want to be personally exposed to the realities of our free-market system. It's much safer to be paid a guaranteed base and predictable bonus, rather than a sum that reflects actual company performance. The "new" shareholder of the future will demand that top management paychecks mirror their company's actual results.

Innovation Fuels Stock Price

Several research studies support a correlation between stock price and successful innovation through new product introduction. Yes, the argument can be made that a myriad of variables drive stock price. However, it is eye-opening to examine the stock price appreciation of companies relative to their competition. What you'll usually find is that companies that consistently launch a steady stream of relatively successful new products and services over a long period experience continued increases in stock prices.

Let's look at some studies that have been conducted on this topic. A 1991 study by Paul Chaney, Timothy Devinney, and Russell Winer, published in "The Impact of New Product Introductions on the Market Value of Firms," in *Journal of Business,* states:

> The aggregate impact of the announcement of a new product was an increase in stock price of approximately .75% over a three-day period. This estimate does not reflect the total value of the product to the firm but is more a measure of the formation of a consensus of the product's value to the firm. As such, it is a lower-bound estimate of the product's value.

Another study published in the *Journal of Political Economy* in 1985 by Ariel Pakes, "On Patents, R&D, and the Stock Market Rate of Return," reports, "On average, unexpected changes in patents and in R&D are associated with quite large changes in the market value of the firm."

These studies are representative of some of the research that has been conducted on innovation's influence on stock price. My own examination of the relationship between stock appreciation and successful new product launches reveals a staggering degree of correlation between the two. Shareholders are already rewarding accomplishments in innovation. They'll do so even more in the future.

During a recent speech I delivered at a strategic planning conference, a vice president of strategic planning challenged me. "Prove to us that successful innovation increases shareholder wealth," he said. "Give us some facts, not your opinion." My response to this rather cynical gentleman was, "I'll be glad to provide some proof, once you prove how a vice president of strategic planning helps a company to increase shareholder wealth." He became silent.

The Market Impact of the CEO

There is no statistically valid research that proves beyond a shadow of a doubt that effective innovation drives up stock price. Similarly, there is no statistical model or software program that calculates the value of a new CEO in determining his or her impact on a company's stock price. But we know, through hundreds of examples, that the CEO does indeed influence stock price.

In most cases, a company's stock will be influenced when a CEO leaves a company or when a new CEO is appointed. The reason is simple. The market is casting its votes in response to the change in CEO. They cast both "support" and "rejection" votes. Shareholders are making a clear-cut judgment statement on the anticipated value that the CEO will bring to the company.

For example, in 1992 the board of directors of General Motors stripped the title of chairman from Robert Stempel. During the 1980s, the company had lost significant domestic auto market share. Shareholders rewarded the actions of the board. GM stock rose 3.5 percent the day they announced the management restructuring. Shareholders had cast a "support" vote for the move. John Smale, former chairman of Procter & Gamble, was appointed acting chairman.

Or look at the impact on Goodyear Tire and Rubber Company's stock when the innovation giant, Stan Gault, left his legendary Rubbermaid to become chairman of Goodyear. Goodyear stock jumped more than 3 share points the day it was announced. Shareholders had clearly been disgruntled with past Goodyear performance, but the stock rose from the 20s to the 60s within three months after Gault joined as chairman. Shareholders do reward innovation leaders. Why? Because they instill an innovation mindset within companies. They increase the productivity and performance of its employee base. They fuel new product revenues. Innovation pays dividends.

The financial community, therefore, interprets and extrapolates a projected value on how well new CEOs will be able to generate future earnings for their companies. Concomitantly, future investors will try to interpret a company's latent power for becoming more successful than competitors at doing innovation. Smart CEOs will become believers that innovation will be counted, scores will be posted, and the winners will be rewarded.

People-Driven Business

Innovation will become a more important factor in investor assessments of a company's value simply because innovation is a people-driven, rather than a process-driven, business function. The most undermanaged and underutilized asset that companies have today is their employee base. My recent book *Values-Based Leadership* depicts the malaise that exists within most U.S. corporations. Employees feel disconnected and alienated from their jobs. For the most part, they receive little personal satisfaction from their ongoing job experiences. They feel demoralized, demeaned, and discouraged. They lack internal motivation and clearly fall short of being highly productive and high-performing employees.

Consequently, most companies today are potentially explosive. People power can either blow up in senior management's face or act as a powerful energy source to catapult a company forward. The issue here is how best to leverage and activate people power. This is the underlying asset that ultimately drives innovation. It's not processes, computer programs, or newfangled speed-to-market gimmicks. It's people. Consequently, innovation is a people-intensive business process.

Therefore, if we are currently underleveraging the asset power of our people, and innovation is a people-intensive process, we should be able to increase innovation performance and new product productivity by better managing and motivating our people.

Thus, we come full circle in the belief that creating an innovation mindset is the vital beginning point for rallying employees and management toward effective innovation. If top executives can set the stage and foster a culture that truly instills an innovation mindset, employees and managers will become more passionate about and committed to their work. If they are encouraged to think more innovatively and are rewarded and recognized for it, they will develop an increased sense of self-identity and self-satisfaction.

The opportunities available to companies to grow their businesses through acquisition and cost reductions are tapering off. The leapfrog competitive advances will not come from trimming the fat more or by relaxing the screens for potential acquisition candidates. Rather, it will come from better utilizing our number-one asset—people—to drive innovation and stimulate the demand side of the business equation through new products, services, marketing approaches, manufacturing processes, and the like.

Corporate America Grows Up

For the past two decades, executives have tried a myriad of constructs to jump-start their company's new products efforts. They've tried a variety of team structures. They've tried a plethora of incentives and rewards. They've even tried the "trim-down/pump-up" approach of downsizing. Accountability has remained foggy. None of these approaches has worked. They haven't worked because, like adolescents, managers haven't been held accountable for innovation results. But the newly awakened shareholder will change all that. Senior management will have to grow up fast, because shareholders will call for it—the innovation age is just around the corner.

To a great extent, the past 20 years have depicted the adolescent stage of new products development in corporate America. Many companies have chosen not to listen to teachings, writings, and proven practices for successful innovation. Excuses like risk aversion, limited capital, and resource constraints abound. But the real reason is that there has not been enough personal motivation or enough vested interest by senior managers to fuel innovation. But that's changing. The innovation teenager is growing up and entering adulthood. This means that the whining will dissipate, the hard work will intensify, and realistic expectations will be matched to available resources.

What might come as a surprise to many CEOs and CFOs is that shareholders will actually want to measure and quantify innovation effectiveness within companies. Shareholders will have equal interest in return on innovation, return on equity, and return on assets (ROA) measures. Consequently, senior managers will pay a lot more attention to determining how new products can impact stock price and increase shareholder wealth. Once that mindset kicks in, our worries about securing top management commitment to innovation will be virtually over.

Seven Forecasted Changes Driving Innovation

We are likely to see many changes that will elevate the importance of innovation management to new heights within companies. I predict seven major changes that will help to establish an innovation mindset:

1. **Shareholders will want annual reports to describe and detail a company's innovation initiatives and returns generated from new product development efforts.** As demonstrated by companies such as Gillette, Amgen, and Apple Computer, even one new product can positively impact stock

prices. Just look at what happened to these companies' stocks after the new Sensor razor, the Epogen drug, and Classic computer were introduced. Increasing shareholder wealth through innovation success will become a 21st-century imperative.

2. **Companies will develop a new financial measurement tool—Return on Innovation (ROI).** This new formula will enable managers to evaluate the total costs spent on innovation across several different departments (including research costs, market research expenditures, new product development costs, and initial launch dollars). Moreover, the returns from new products will be calculated on a five-year rolling basis to provide an ongoing ROI of a company's new products portfolio against which to measure progress.

3. **Innovation will be established as a separate yet integrated function within companies.** In the future, we'll see more organizations with an autonomous innovation department. It won't be an ad hoc committee, temporary task force or semi-dedicated team of managers. In contrast, the innovation department will be staffed with its own cadre of permanent professionals with multi-functional backgrounds. This department will be interdependent with other functional areas and will help to facilitate the integration of resources. Innovation will receive its own career-track status.

4. **New products and innovation managers will be viewed as potential COOs and CEOs.** The skills necessary to cope with the increasingly complex nature of innovation will prepare innovation leaders to become effective organizational leaders. Innovation will be used as a training ground for future corporate leaders. The very essence of innovation management will call for a Renaissance person with a broad range of strong interpersonal and motivational skills, similar to the attributes necessary for an effective CEO.

5. **A new type of market research will focus on consumer problems and needs identification prior to idea generation.** Need-intensity and problem-solution research will explore the fundamental values held by and behaviors of consumers. A series of idea or problem-solving brainstorming sessions can then follow. A problems and needs form of market research, combined with an intense understanding of consumer norms and values, will be better able to calibrate need intensity for screening potential new products.

6. **Larger financial investments will be made in radical innovation and technology breakthroughs as the proliferation of line extension and "me-too" new products dramatically declines.** Managers will recognize that sinking more and more dollars into incremental innovation will not yield returns worth the investments. The perceived risk of failure for line extensions is low, but the rate of return is usually equally low. Radical innovation will earn the bulk of the innovation investment dollars.

7. **Companies will establish dramatically new compensation incentives for innovation managers, departments, and teams.** These incentives will enable individuals to personally invest in a new product within a company. In turn, employees might lose their investments or receive high returns based on the performance of the product in the marketplace over a five-year or other investment period.

We are rapidly approaching the Innovation Age. As shareholders continue to recognize the role that innovation can play in fueling profitable growth, management will be forced to enter into young adulthood. Of course, growing up isn't easy, and sometimes maturation occurs a lot later than expected. In the case of innovation, growing up has required a couple of extra decades.

Ask Shareholders about Their Expectations

Top management must determine shareholder goals, objectives, and expectations. Shareholder expectations can no longer be assumed. U.S. companies have consistently made fallacious assumptions about shareholder perceptions, needs, and wants. Similar to domineering parents who presume they always know what's best for their child, patronizing executives erroneously assume that they know what's best for the stockholder. They don't. They need to ask them.

Shareholder input should be sought out and valued by top managers. They need to influence the development of long-term financial goals and strategic objectives. Although myopic executives often profess to know more than shareholders about their companies, that attitude is part of the problem. Shareholders aren't informed or educated enough. They are excluded from the formation of a company's growth strategy. This must change. Shareholder views on innovation and their desire and intentions about long-term investments should be factored into the strategy-setting equation.

When was the last time you received a survey from the company you owned stock in? Probably never. And yet this can be a compelling source of information to help support and validate an innovation strategy. I know many of you are probably thinking, "Shareholders will obviously want to maximize their returns in the short term." I disagree. If you make the effort to learn what shareholders want, you might find that they have a far greater interest in long-term yields than in the traditionally viewed 90-day, short-term earnings increases.

The message is to find out—one way or another. Let shareholders contribute to and help define your future investment posture for innovation. In a *Business Week* editorial, "Annual Meetings Don't Have to Be a Waste of Everybody's Time" (May 10, 1993), Judith H. Dobrzynski writes, "Often, as few as a dozen institutions own 40% to 50% of a company—they have the right to tell management what's on their mind." And, in turn, management needs to listen, absorb, integrate, and act on this information, not just to disregard it as uninformed opinions of outside shareholders.

Does the Financial Community Support Innovation?

The glib response to this question is, "Only if innovation yields dividend increases and quarterly earnings upswings." But shareholders and even financial analysts are changing to some degree. They are recognizing the value of a company that is committed to ongoing and consistent investments in innovation. Witness the stock appreciation track record of companies like 3M, Motorola, Amgen, Owens-Corning, Rubbermaid, and Pfizer, each of which has increased its annual stock prices by an average of more than 15 percent during the past five years. Each of these companies has coincidentally spent more than 4 percent of sales on R&D. Each has been able to instill an innovation mindset.

The reason shareholders are paying far more attention to innovation is, in part, demonstrated by new initial public offering (IPO) stocks. Many new stocks more than double in price within the first year of their initial offering. Shareholders reward companies for new, innovative products and services. Likewise, companies that continue to be successful at long-term innovation and generate a balanced new products portfolio are being recognized as attractive picks for investors' stock portfolios.

Skeptics will ask, "How can you prove that stock price is driven by innovation?" Look at the stock performance during the past three years of Hartmarx, Borden, and Greyhound. Their stocks have remained flat or headed south during this time. Can you name one—just one—new product or service that any of these companies has launched in three years? Answer: No, because they haven't.

The Need for an Innovation Index

Return on Innovation will become a major benchmark of interest to the financial community. The investing community does take innovativeness into account when evaluating a company. However, as many have stated in our conversations with them, the difficulty is the lack of innovation metrics. As one Merrill Lynch analyst stated:

> How can you measure innovation? And worse yet, innovation potential? The intangibility of the innovation process and uncertainty about its components make it very difficult to evaluate.

Interestingly, several analysts we interviewed felt that some type of innovation indices or benchmarks, an Innovation Score or Innovation Index, would be helpful tools for assessing the innovation potential of a company. Over time, these indices could be validated by tracking the tangible results generated through innovation. The hard part is coming up with the initial list of variables that will correlate to innovation success.

Chapter 8 presents several new metrics for evaluating innovation. These indices might open up new avenues for the financial community to better understand and be better equipped to project innovation potential within companies. An analyst from Fidelity Investments who manages a $1 billion mutual fund says:

> Intelligent, customer-based innovation always drives up the market value of a firm, but *inconsistent* innovation causes price volatility and downward fluctuations.

Consistency Is Key

The message here is clear: Innovation needs to be done consistently. It can't be turned on and off. Maybe the financial community already does recognize this to a greater extent than some top executives are willing to admit. If you plan to use innovation as a growth strategy, then stick with it. You need to innovate continuously in order for innovation to play a positive role in driving up stock prices.

Another analyst we interviewed described innovation with great insight. He very wisely defined innovation in a way that talks more about the people, process, and mindset than bottom-line profits. He acknowledged that the profits will come if the key components of innovation are in place.

> Innovation is an intimate process that can and should involve everyone in the company. Integral components of the innovation process most often include: (1) An "open," less bureaucratic culture; anti-hierarchical organization structures, (2) effective communication, (3) team focus and compensation to counter individual insecurity, and (4) inculcation of a sense of purpose and pride in employees across the board.

Many investors today use informal, subjective measures to determine and judge a company's level of innovation effectiveness. Moreover, the criteria they use differ widely. However, they do tend to share one common view:

> Innovation is valued to the extent that it presents an opportunity to strengthen a company's competitive position.

This is why the consistency issue is valued by financial investors. One new innovation alone can indeed contribute additional earnings to a company's bottom line, but it will have minimal impact on a company's long-term value. Consistent and continuous innovation, on the other hand, can greatly contribute to and directly influence the long-term value of a firm. As presented in **Exhibit 4.1**, other investors share similar thoughts.

The challenge then is to evaluate two aspects of innovation simultaneously: (1) the profit performance of new products launched and (2) the potential of an organization to effectively innovate over time. It's the combination of both of these benchmarks that can be used to determine the extent to which a company's value will be impacted by innovation. As summarized well by a 20-year veteran stock broker:

Exhibit 4.1

Additional Insights from the Investment Community

"A solid, valid measure of innovation would be of great interest—but none exists."

"Innovation is mainly an intangible and subjective measure, which is particularly difficult to quantify given that it is largely based on perception rather than hard facts."

"Choosing the indicators would be no easy task. A given investment in R&D could yield very different results based on the personnel involved, the department focus, methodologies followed, and the industry."

"Perhaps more insightful than given investments in R&D or the percentage of revenues which come from new products would be an understanding of the management and organization. This brings us to the chicken and egg paradox: Which holds more importance: an innovative product or an innovative organization?"

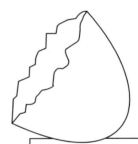

Product

"Snapple did a great job of capturing the non-alcoholic off-the-shelf drink segment."

"Tangible products make the biggest impression on me, rather than the organization."

"Even though Microsoft is huge, they remain innovative risk-takers."

"I can truly know a product but I can't gauge an organization."

Organizations

"Snapple hasn't done much lately with the exception of introducing new flavors."

"An innovative organization can keep introducing new products while developing new defensive techniques."

"Microsoft keeps enhancing Windows, rather than building doors."

"Products come and go, organizations persist."

You can't sail a boat on yesterday's wind; and while some market inertia persists after a successful new product innovation, companies that fail to continually innovate will take a beating in the marketplace. Expectations run wild when the market gets excited about the prospects of continued innovation, thus placing a burden on the innovating company to continue as the innovation leader in their given segment or niche.

The common theme clearly emerging from the financial community is the need for continuity and consistency of innovation. The risk that a company runs is that once you begin innovation, you can't afford to quit doing it.

The Coming Innovation Revolution

During the past century, we have evolved through three major business revolutions: agricultural, industrial, and informational. We are about to enter the Innovation Revolution. Every turn of a century seems to stimulate a surge of new inventions, new technologies, and new advancements. It happened in the late 1790s, 1890s, and is showing signs of the same in the 1990s. The timing is not just coincidence. A new century sparks a rebirth of creative thinking, sets the stage for new hopes, and stimulates new ideas.

The emergence of innovation is inevitable. We have cost-reduced and reengineered ourselves to death. It's hard to believe that companies can get more cost-efficient, productive, and lean and mean. The fat has already been trimmed—we're now down to the bone.

Companies will not be able to sustain consistent earnings increases without effectively managing innovation. Commensurate with that will be the dire need for top executives to increase the amount of time that they personally devote to innovation. This does not mean that you should be intervening in decision making or usurping accountability from new products teams. It does, however, suggest that you need to play the role of servant to and advocate of innovation. You will view innovation as one of your most valuable tools for stimulating consumer demand and erecting competitive barriers.

Servant of Innovation

The role of servant means exactly that, to serve others involved in innovation but provide them with the funding, people resources, and rewards structure to be able to do new products right. If a new products team has to "tin cup" and panhandle their way through corporate corridors begging for resources and capital, this won't foster innovation.

Advocate for Innovation

Innovation must become a first-class citizen and drop its second-class citizenship. It must be elevated to a function with as much stature as finance, manufacturing, sales, or marketing. It can no longer be relegated and delegated down to the bottom of an organization. Becoming an advocate of innovation means supporting its endeavors, espousing its benefits, and, most importantly, believing in its value.

Until top executives believe that innovation can help increase stock price, motivate employees, retain current customers, and attract new customers, it will be difficult for others to become innovation advocates. Removing bureaucratic barriers and encouraging diversity on new products teams are two specific ways to serve and show advocacy. Enabling employees to challenge the status quo, defining a business or product category in an expanded and visionary way, and tolerating failures will help them to believe that innovation does count and is supported by the company.

The Government Must Help

As shareholders shout louder for innovation, companies will ask forcefully for help from our government. Forming a new government task force or committee to study innovation is not the answer. However, following are four potential ways in which the U.S. government could support more innovation and encourage companies to invest in it:

- **Change the Tax Laws.** Companies should be financially rewarded, not penalized, for investment in innovation.

- **Create a Secretary of Innovation.** This new cabinet position would be responsible for developing programs and initiatives to stimulate a resurgence in innovation. Defense research, which has continued at an accelerated speed, should be converted to commercial applications. This source of new technology and innovation for business is yet untapped.

- **Establish National Innovation Awards.** Such awards would recognize innovation superiority and create innovation benchmarks that companies could use to monitor the effectiveness of their own innovation efforts. This might be similar in nature to the national Malcolm Baldrige Award for quality.

- **Form a Global Council on Innovation Competitiveness.** This would include worldwide leaders from the top 50 global companies. The United States would initiate this endeavor, but its representation would come from around the world. Think of it as a United Nations Security Council for innovating rather than peacekeeping.

Innovation Pays for Itself

Companies that take the risk and are willing to invest in new-to-the-world, new-to-the-century, and new-to-the-company products are the ones that will generate the big returns. Investing in line extensions and flankers requires less risk, but it doesn't provide significant financial benefits. In a recent study, we found that in the "best" new products companies, 39 percent of their new products were either new-to-the-world or new-to-the-company, in contrast to only 23 percent for the "rest" category of companies. (See **Exhibit 4.2**.)

Exhibit 4.2

Percentage of New Product Revenue by New Product Type

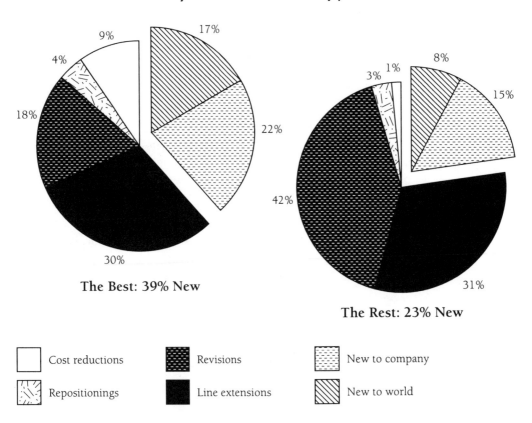

The Best: 39% New

The Rest: 23% New

☐ Cost reductions	▦ Revisions	▨ New to company
⊞ Repositionings	■ Line extensions	▧ New to world

Source: "Winning New Product and Service Practices for the 1990s," Kuczmarski & Associates, Inc.

The finding is that innovation pays for itself. The higher returns come from pursuing the higher-risk, higher-investment forms of innovation. Shareholders in the future will pay for innovation, too.

This chapter concludes with a reminder of the value and importance of an innovation mindset. Leo Burnett USA is a great example of an advertising company with an innovation mindset. The core competency of this business is creativity, and the company has maintained a philosophy that supports openness and yields superior advertising. As David Olsen, Group Research Director for Leo Burnett, states, "The only totally surefire way to reduce the failure rate of new products to zero is to just stop launching them."

In summary, shareholders will accelerate innovation. Their thirst for it will intensify. Their desire to see it will increase. Publicly traded companies will have virtually no alternative but to innovate. The age of innovation has indeed arrived.

Innovation Checklist: Fifteen Principles of Successful New Product Marketing*

Product Development/Positioning

1. Distinguish your product from competition in a consumer-relevant way.
2. Capitalize on key corporate competencies/brand strengths.
3. Develop/market to people's needs and habits.
4. Market to long-term trends, not fads.
5. Don't ignore research, but don't be paralyzed by it.

Introductory Strategy

6. Make sure your timing is right.
7. Be a marketing leader, not a distant follower.
8. Offer a real value to consumers.

9. Determine product's short- and long-term sales potential.

10. Gain legitimacy and momentum for the brand.

11. Give the trade as good a deal as the consumer.

Communicating the Product Proposition

12. Clearly define, understand, and talk to your target.

13. Develop and communicate a distinctive and appealing brand character and stick to it.

14. Spend competitively and efficiently, behind a relevant proposition.

Follow-Up Strategy

15. Make sure the customer is satisfied and stays that way.

*David Olsen, Group Research Director, Leo Burnett USA.

chapter five

Preparing to Spread the Innovation Gospel

Energizing Your Personal Commitment

The *first* task of business leaders . . . is to create an environment in which there can flourish not only individual genius, but more important, the collective capacities of other people in the organization.

—Abram T. Collier

Chief Executive Officer is a fitting title for the leader of innovation. One definition of *chief* is the head or leader of a tribe, family, or clan. This is an appropriate description in the context of effective innovation. A hierarchical or autocratic management style will stifle innovation. The person ultimately leading the innovation process should adopt a nurturing approach.

If top executives view the innovation organization as a family or clan, they foster an environment in which employees are treated with mutual respect, trust, and caring. Likewise, the "tribe" members are free to be more participatory and results-oriented. But, before you can instill in others a proactive mindset that stimulates innovation, you need to internalize your own conviction and belief in innovation. You need to find and cultivate innovation passion.

Sustaining Innovation Over Time

Financial results are probably the best way to develop conviction about the need to innovate and an intrinsic endorsement of innovation. Because you like to deal with numbers, you trust numbers; you feel comfortable with numbers. You've been conditioned that way. And, indeed, the numbers will materialize if innovation is funded, performed, and managed consistently. The problem is that it will take time. Most corporate and entrepreneurial CEOs are impatient. They want to see a cause and effect, instantly. That won't happen with innovation. Its gestation, development, and maturation phases take many months to come to fruition. So you need to find a way to establish a sustained belief in innovation that will last through these evolutionary phases and give you emotional stamina and staying power.

The best way to acquire this requisite stamina, and avoid pulling the innovation plug when your numbers slip one quarter, is to "pump up" your own personal conviction for innovation. If you are able to develop a trust in innovation, a solid understanding of its benefits, and an internal voice that tells you it's the right thing to do, you'll be well on your way toward internalizing a desire to make innovation work. Within two to three years, your company's financial results will begin to be positively influenced by the innovation mindset that you've cultivated within your company. You'll soon have some evidence that innovation was a smart investment. It will then be easier to keep investing in and supporting it. But the first few years are the most difficult time to stay on course.

Hold the Reins Yourself

One way to build this conviction is to set innovation as your own number-one priority. Keep it a top-of-mind issue and activity. Don't delegate it all away. Top executives can make or break innovation by the level of personal interest they show. The desire for effective innovation must develop within you before you can go about trying to create an innovation mindset in others.

As the ultimate innovation leader, you truly do have the power—both authority and financial power—to change your organization and stimulate an innovation mindset. But you must begin by building your own conviction in innovation. It does become a personal process, one that mandates an internalized desire to make innovation happen based on your belief in the benefits that can accrue from it. If you are still a "doubting Thomas" and are unsure about whether innovation is the right strategy for your company, you need to change your opinion now!

Stay Ahead of the Pack

The innovation train has already left the station. Don't be the last one to jump on board. By the turn of the century, U.S. companies will once again be taking the global lead in advancing new state-of-the-art technologies and launching a steady stream of new-to-the-world products and services. Innovation won't be done the way it was in the past. Our future leaders will demonstrate an ability to motivate employees to think creatively and integrate an innovation mindset into the basic fabric of daily business life.

Make sure that you're not left behind, with your competitors pulling out ahead. Innovation's time has come. As reengineering and cost-reduction initiatives are reaching a point of diminishing returns, innovation is just getting itself in gear. Don't be the leader sitting in the dark while your competitive colleagues discover the light that innovation can bring to profitable future growth.

Personal Benefits of Innovation

You can benefit personally from an aggressive pursuit of innovation. You will enhance your own credibility and leave your mark on your organization by using innovation to drive your company's strategy. By creating an innovation mindset throughout your organization, you'll have a multitude of employees who are focused on generating new ideas, new approaches, and new services. What this potentially means is an exponential increase in the number of new sources of innovation. Rather than having a few scattered teams focused on new product development, you can leverage an entire work force to bring innovation to the forefront of every functional activity. By bringing innovation into all functions and disciplines within a company, you can maximize the overall performance output of your employee base. This, in turn, will further accelerate your ability to gain competitive advantage and increase future profits.

Talk Is Cheap—Innovation Conviction Counts

Talk is cheap. About the worst thing you can do is to talk about innovation and convey a lack of genuineness or sincerity in the message. Employees will very quickly pick up on this. Unless there is a foundation of internal conviction toward innovation, the message will be viewed as unfounded lip service. A lot of second-guessing will commence as employees try to figure out what you *really* want. They'll discern that while you are trying to lip-sync the words "innovation mindset," in reality you're humming a different tune. Then a lot of wasted time is spent on trying to "name that tune." This causes confusion and frustration. So, say what you mean. If you don't buy into the benefits of innovation, then say so. But don't preach its merits unless you truly become an apostle of innovation.

Suppose you announce your desire for innovation and then begin to pressure managers to cut their budgets. This might very well signal to them that they need to be spending more time on the existing business rather than worrying about future projects. So, the first step is to measure your own level of innovation conviction. (See **Exhibit 5.1.**) Next, you will determine how best to communicate it and to ensure that there are no mixed messages. Once you've done this, you should monitor the "vibes" you are emitting about your attitudes toward innovation. It's then up to you to determine how to gain more conviction and develop the action steps to get there.

The first five questions in Exhibit 5.1 are aimed at reminding you about the positive experiences you've had or are aware others have had with innovation. If you "know" that innovation can work, you're well on your way toward a high desire-intensity for instilling an innovation mindset within your company. The last five questions are geared to determine your company's degree of readiness to accept innovation as a problem-solving tool or as a way to leverage core competencies. The combination of these motivators provides both an offensive and defensive impetus for recognizing the potential merits of innovation. Once you've internalized the upside, positive benefits of innovation as well as its solutions-generating capabilities, your desire-intensity for it will increase.

Innovation as a Value

The conviction for innovation, however, should go beyond exploiting its power to gain competitive advantage or fueling future growth by addressing strategic roles. Creativity, invention, and the birthing of newness should permeate every company as a fundamental philosophy and core value.

More than 40 years ago, in 1953, Abram T. Collier, a former chairman of New England Mutual Life Insurance Company, wrote

Exhibit 5.1

Measuring Your Innovation Conviction

To facilitate your self-discovery about your conviction to innovation, please complete the following quiz. It will help you determine how you and your company feel about innovation. Score the accuracy of each statement as follows:

0 = Not at all accurate
5 = Somewhat accurate
10 = Accurate

_____ 1. My company has had a major new product success within the past three years that had a significant positive impact on growth.

_____ 2. New products have expanded the size of the category within which many of our product lines compete.

_____ 3. At least one of our key competitors has been successful at using innovation to substantially increase its competitive advantage.

_____ 4. I am personally aware of several other industries that have grown through successful innovation.

_____ 5. Other senior and functional managers within the company have expressed interest in strengthening innovation and share a belief in its potential value.

_____ 6. Recent acquisitions and strategic alliances made by our company have not been as successful as originally forecast.

_____ 7. Market share increases in recent years have been modest, at best.

_____ 8. Margins of existing product lines continue to fall prey to fierce price competition and consequently show signs of erosion.

_____ 9. We've reduced our cost structures, have already streamlined our work force, and have reengineered our processes.

_____ 10. Our company has invested in R&D, which has resulted in some unique technology advancements that have not yet been fully exploited or leveraged.

(continued)

Exhibit 5.1 *(continued)*

Measuring Your Innovation Conviction

Scoring:

60 and above   Your innovation desire-intensity is high. You are ready to instill innovation in your employees.

40–59   Your innovation desire-intensity is moderate. You should explore ways to develop it further.

Less than 40   You probably have a low level of interest or belief in innovation. Do not pursue a strategy that includes innovation as a cornerstone until you increase your own conviction.

"Business Leadership and a Creative Society," in *Harvard Business Review.* He stated:

> I put forward this simple proposition; that our society is a creative society; that its prime objective is its creativeness; and that, since creative accomplishment is the actual day-to-day goal of modern business, it is also the keystone of our business philosophy.

His words are an excellent description of a still applicable philosophy for guiding us into the next century. It's our responsibility as leaders to create newness. So, above and beyond all the important business strategy reasons to innovate, it's also part of our job to try to make society better. Creativity, when directed at problem solving, can often provide long-term benefits to society and its members.

Less Focus on Obsolescence

Too often, we focus on intentional obsolescence. We're too concerned that our new idea, invention, or product should have built-in "failure" mechanisms that will stimulate repurchase by consumers. We want the consumer to have to repurchase our product frequently. Well, let's not worry so much about that. Instead, let's focus on creating the best solution possible to address problems in a new way. Let's develop the very highest quality products and services possible. Let's err on the side of innovation superiority. It's our societal as well as our business responsibility to do so.

Developing All Employees

Collier argued convincingly that business leaders should instill creativity throughout an organization so that every employee thinks creatively. To accomplish this type of environment, Collier proposed four factors that need to be present to evoke creativity:

1. Differences and diversity must exist between individuals and groups.
2. Individuals need to understand each other in depth.
3. Goals must be matched with resources.
4. The directing force in a creative society is the faith of its members in individual growth.

Collier's four factors are a wonderful statement on how innovation and creativity require a balance of conflict, struggle, understanding, sharing, and cooperation. These are attributes that are not contradictory. They provide electricity and spark innovation. For many years, I have seen that tension can generate positive results. Conflict can be healthy. As long as people trust their organization and its leadership, they will feel comfortable to experience individual and group conflict. This provides a give and take, a need to reach and build consensus, which often helps to solidify a team or group.

Forget the Suggestion Box

Suggestion boxes for new ideas don't work. I can't imagine anything more impersonal and void of individualistic expression than an empty box hanging on the wall in a corridor. Why should any employee bother to take the time to submit new product ideas to a box? Will the box talk to them when they submit their piece of paper? Will someone call them on the phone and thank them? Or, do the instructions on the box inform the idea generator to submit their ideas anonymously?

The message here is that innovation must be a personal process. It must capture the hearts and emotional fabric of an individual. It can't be sterile or impersonal. Creativity must be captivating. Innovation must be motivating. Developing your own conviction for innovation will be a critical step toward breathing some passion for innovation into your employees. And oh, by the way, tear down the suggestion box, if you currently have one.

Ask Not What Innovation Can Do for You, Ask What You Can Do for Innovation

If you have an intense conviction in the value of innovation, then you are ready for some stage-setting activities to spark the development of an innovation mindset.

Develop a Personal Rationale for Accelerating Innovation

Writing a statement about your personal support for innovation will help to further strengthen your own conviction in innovation as well as provide a reason for other key managers to believe in it. The rationale should include reasons related to the company goals, category dynamics, competitive responses, shareholder objectives, and customer and employee satisfaction. Each of these rationale categories should be addressed in a way that describes the role you want innovation to play in addressing these issues. The reasons must be specific and actionable. An example of a personal rationale statement is shown in **Exhibit 5.2.**

Read about Innovation and Write a "Before Innovation and After" Article

You need to become familiar with some of the latest thinking on innovation and new product development. My book *Managing New Products: The Power of Innovation* will serve as a "how-to" primer on new products development. There is a list of many other excellent books and articles on the topic at the end of this book. The key is to get several of these readings and get through all of them within a 30-day period. Take some notes, and jot down the ideas you think are most applicable to your own situation. Engulf yourself in the topic area. This will increase your own confidence and comfort level, which in all likelihood will enhance your innovation desire-intensity.

The idea of developing an article for publication on the topic of innovation's impact on your own company has three potential benefits:

1. **It will enable you to think about what innovation has done for your company.** It forces you to get your hands dirty on the topic by analyzing the effects of innovation on company growth. So, the first benefit of writing an article is to enhance your own understanding of innovation's benefits.

2. **The article will be a great internal communications tool to distribute to all of your employees.** It will make a terrific conviction statement to everyone involved in innovation as well as to the whole organization that you really do care about it.

Exhibit 5.2

Personal Rationale Statement

I want our innovation efforts to generate a portfolio of new products that, five years from now, will provide $100 million in new revenues and at least $40 million in incremental profits. I want some of our new products to provide us with a way to enter at least one new market and some others to enable us to attract a new customer segment. I'd like a portion of those new products to leverage two of our core technologies as well as further capitalize on our expansive distribution network.

I believe that some of our future new-to-the-world products (and I do want some of those radically new types) should enable us to leapfrog ahead of our primary competitor and simultaneously increase our stock price by at least 20–25 percent in the year of launch. A few other new products should help to expand the size of the category.

I want to establish an innovation mindset throughout the company to enrich the job satisfaction of my employees. I want them to know that I do accept failure as part of the innovation process. I want them to know how much I support, endorse, and reinforce their efforts. I want innovation to be a tool to motivate them and to foster higher dosages of creativity in their daily thinking.

I want innovation to position us in the minds of our customers as a progressive, customer-oriented, innovative leader in the marketplace. I want our customers to see, sense, and experience nothing but the highest quality from the new products we launch.

I want to accelerate our innovation initiatives to better enable us to achieve all of these things to make our company one that its employees, shareholders, and customers can be proud of. I believe in innovation.

3. **Top executives' views** *should* **be published in external publications.** This article could be enclosed in a mailing to shareholders as well as key analysts in the financial community. It could also be turned into an op-ed piece for publication in a local or national newspaper.

There are many ways to leverage an article on innovation within several constituencies. It's well worth your time to write one.

Schedule Regular Innovation Lunches

There is not enough information exchange between leaders. Assuming that your egos can take it, schedule four luncheons each year with other top executives to talk about innovation. You can discuss their challenges with it, approaches that have and haven't worked well for them, their attitudes and feelings about innovation, and the like. Most likely, talking with others about innovation will heighten your awareness of the common problems, issues, questions, doubts, and concerns that exist among most executives. This will reassure you that you're not alone in confronting these issues. You will realize that most executives are dealing with similar questions facing innovation effectiveness. You can swap "war stories" and learn from each other.

Innovate Yourself

So what can you do if you don't have an enthusiasm for or interest in innovation? Well, first, you need to re-read your strategic plan to identify whether innovation is integral to achieving your business goals. It it's not, you're off the hook. Dropping an interest in innovation is just fine. However, if innovation is needed to achieve your strategy, then you need to warm up to innovation quickly and build some personal conviction for it.

To do this, you need to self-administer your own dose of whatever it takes to energize yourself about innovation. You need to be optimistic and buoyant about the potential of innovation—of what it can do for you, your company, your employees, your shareholders, and your customers. The quizzes, techniques, tools, ideas, and perspectives presented in this book should help stimulate a greater understanding of innovation. Usually, increased understanding fosters greater motivation. But, you will also need to undertake some initiatives that work best for you personally.

How do you re-charge your batteries, develop a fresh perspective, renew your own commitment, and convince yourself that innovation is the right thing to do? You do it by motivating yourself, by building a fascination for and curiosity about innovation, and by becoming more aware of how it works. This is difficult to do. It's a bit like trying to hold on to fog—just when you think you might have it, it's gone. The following tips might help you become a stronger innovation "believer" and eventually be able to spread the innovation gospel.

Become Involved in Innovation

Being involved in innovation is essential for activating your own awareness, understanding, and excitement for new products and innovation:

- Attend some new products team meetings.

- Visit the technology labs.

- Take a new products engineer to lunch.

- Join the innovation steering committee.

- Have quarterly breakfasts with each new products team leader.

Stick your nose in things, but probe gently. Don't become a "butt-in-ski," but rather an interested and engaging leader of innovation. Get your hands dirty. Talk about it, read about it, and do it. Involvement with innovation will help to spark greater interest in it and conviction for it.

Build a Shared Innovation Vision with Your Management Team

Engage in a two-way dialogue with your management team about the benefits, challenges, and goals of innovation at your company. Your key managers will have many additional perspectives and insights that will help you further develop a self-affirmation for innovation. Granted, some of these conversations will gravitate to gripes and complaints about the company's innovation approaches and practices being taken. However, remain proactive and try to turn even those issues into constructive lessons learned, which can heighten your understanding of the complexity of innovation.

Eventually, you'll want to have several candid discussions with your entire management team about the role of innovation at your company and the approaches you want to take to accelerate it. You'll need to take the reins, though, for creating a shared innovation vision. Again, this will help to build your own belief in its value.

Discuss Innovation with External Constituencies

Talk about your company's stance on innovation at press conferences, at shareholder meetings, at analyst meetings, with your financial lenders, at speeches you are giving, and at conferences you're attending. Make a committed statement to these constituencies about how important innovation is to the future success of your company. Tell them about some of the specific actions you're taking to ensure that it works well. Tell them what your expected returns on innovation will be and why they should pay more attention to this new ROI benchmark. Make them feel that you really are committed to innovation. This, of course, will be self-affirming to you and subconsciously increase your own personal commitment, which you will want to live up to. You've said that you will create an innovation mindset. You keep your promises! It's a good start for further bolstering your own conviction.

Announce Your Innovation Intentions Internally

Talk about your commitment and dedication to innovation at employee meetings. Write an article for your company newsletter that outlines the action steps and new initiatives that you are undertaking to help support innovation. Develop an "Innovation Creed" that defines the values and norms that you believe should guide innovation endeavors and behaviors.

Ask your employees to give you their ideas on ways you can be a more effective innovation leader. Solicit their inputs on ways to change the new products development process. Make a statement about the role of innovation in your annual report. Let your shareholders know your intentions, too.

Discuss innovation up and down the organization—don't limit your dialogue only to your direct reports. Write an occasional impromptu memo to some new products team member about his or her valuable contributions to the innovation effort. Convey a spirited, can-do mindset about innovation to others in the organization. Again, these externally stated messages often build your internal conviction.

In short, you need to commit yourself to innovation in a way that prevents you from backing out of it. You need a bit of personal commitment-making to ensure that you don't get cold feet in a few months. Although I fully recognize how difficult it is to remain optimistic and buoyant about innovation when you continually hear gripes, hassles, and complaints from employees involved with innovation, hang in there. Do whatever is required to put yourself in a positive frame of mind. Give yourself a pep talk. But give yourself permission to lose your optimism occasionally, too. That's understandable. You have a myriad of challenges to deal with. Make an effort to re-energize yourself, jump back on the innovation bandwagon, and continue to spread the gospel of innovation.

The Innovation Creed

If your desire for increased innovation is already relatively high, then read the Innovation Creed at the end of this chapter and check off those statements that you currently believe in and support. If you believe at least 10 out of the 15 innovation beliefs, then you already have enough insight about innovation to maintain a strong personal conviction.

The issue here is two-fold: First, as a top executive you must be internally committed to innovation. Second, you must understand the underlying benefits of innovation and act in a way that mirrors your stated conviction.

Share the Innovation Creed with others in your company. Ask them to identify how many of the 15 beliefs they endorse and buy into. Compare the responses from four or five of your managers. Examine the similarities and differences, and discuss them at an innovation lunch or breakfast.

Building conviction and internalizing your desire-intensity for innovation is the prerequisite for creating an innovation mindset. You must remember the daily impact that you have on your organization. As a result, your words about innovation must be supported by concrete actions. You must remember to link the two. If you espouse only words with no actions, everyone in your organization will very quickly know it. You'll need to monitor yourself to maintain a bridge between your innovation words and actions.

Moreover, use whatever approach works for you to get yourself in a positive, can-do frame of mind toward innovation. Be conscious of what motivates you, and self-administer your own dose of it. Try using total immersion from time to time. Get acquainted with innovation. Understand it, discuss it, think about it, and talk about it. You have the power to unleash an innovation mindset throughout your company. Make sure *you* adopt one first.

Innovation Checklist: The Innovation Creed

1. I believe innovative new products and services are integral to my company's future success.
2. I believe I control the future success of innovation for my company.
3. I believe new-to-the-world products can be our most valued currency.
4. I believe successful internal innovation will yield greater returns than equally risky acquisitions.
5. I believe long-term investments in innovation will yield profitable returns if managed correctly.
6. I believe innovation will pay for itself and generate high returns if a balanced new products portfolio is maintained.
7. I believe that quantity of new products is as important as their quality.
8. I believe new solutions to existing problems will provide big-hit new product opportunities.
9. I believe that I am one of the biggest assets or most impenetrable barriers that can make or break innovation.
10. I believe that an effective innovation mindset can motivate my employees to perform better and be more productive.
11. I believe that the death or success of innovation lies directly in my hands.

12. I believe that measuring return on innovation is as important as measuring return on equity.

13. I believe that failure is an intrinsic component of innovation, and I accept that.

14. I believe that maintaining a positive, proactive, and buoyant attitude about innovation is critical for morale.

15. I believe innovation should be one of my top five priorities and remain on my to-do list.

chapter six

Laying the Foundation of an Innovation Mindset
The Eight Building Blocks

Innovation is both conceptual and perceptual. Purposeful, systematic innovation begins with the analysis of potential opportunities.

— Peter F. Drucker, *Innovation and Entrepreneurship*

This chapter presents the eight building blocks for laying the foundation of an innovation mindset. It provides a snapshot of the essential components of a successful innovation program. You will need to apply lots of "leadership glue" to hold the building blocks in place. You'll need to hold an innovation summit (see Chapter 7), create a shared leadership innovation team, and measure your returns on innovation (see Chapter 8).

To be successful at creating an innovation mindset, you have to look your organization straight in the eye and say, "I'm going to change the way we've done innovation." Making a few improvements to the way innovation has always been done won't work. You need to change the paradigm. Trying harder and doing things better isn't enough. The eight building blocks of innovation provide a solid base upon which an organization can structure itself.

If the blocks are properly assembled, they'll provide the raw ingredients for a successful batch of innovation. But be careful—there is an art to mixing those ingredients together and cooking them until done. Instinct and intuition are part of innovation.

The Three Innovation Platforms

There are three platforms upon which the building blocks are assembled:

1. Planning for innovation
2. Defining the development process
3. Crafting a holistic innovation organization

These three platforms are interconnected. Once the eight building blocks are assembled on these platforms, you'll have a fortified structure to support an innovation mindset. I'll now discuss each of the building blocks. The overall set of blocks and platforms are depicted in **Exhibit 6.1.**

1. Create an Innovation Vision and Blueprint

An innovation vision enables a company to see beyond its current business to the one it wants to evolve into. This vision depicts the role

Exhibit 6.1

The Eight Building Blocks of Innovation

Planning for Innovation

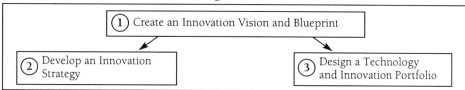

Defining the Development Process

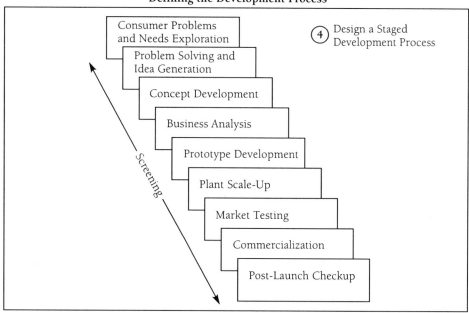

Crafting a Holistic Innovation Organization

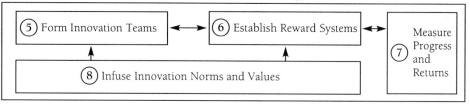

that creating newness will play in reshaping the future appearance of the company. It describes the long-term mission and purpose of innovation. It identifies how innovation will change the strategic direction and portfolio mix of products and services sold. The innovation vision will capture the way you want current and future employees to perceive the company five to ten years from now.

The Innovation Vision and the Corporate Vision

The corporate vision statement should be closely linked to the innovation vision. They should support and reinforce each other. But the two are different and should stand as two distinct documents. The corporate vision articulates the purpose of the organization—why it's in business. It describes the role of a company as an economic entity. An example of a corporate vision:

> **Corporate Vision**
> To be recognized as the global leader in electronic equipment that satisfies consumers' leisure needs. To achieve aggressive returns to our shareholders by continuing robust growth.

The innovation vision, in contrast, describes what you want the company to become in the future. It explains how innovation will be used as a catalyst for getting there. It sets up the end-point that you are trying to reach through innovation initiatives. It should crystallize the desired future image of the company that you'll want to project. It's perfectly fine for the innovation vision to be no more than one or two paragraphs. An example of an innovation vision:

> **Innovation Vision**
> We will effectively use innovation to reshape our company from how we know it today. Within ten years we will be recognized as the global leader of home leisure and recreational electronic equipment products. Consumers will have

virtually no reason to leave their homes for recreation. Our unique and totally new-to-the-world products will transform the way we currently think about leisure and participate in recreation. Team sports will still be played, but via electronic media.

We will be known as the "Fun at Home" company. We will guarantee our product quality as well as the total satisfaction of each consumer who wants to gain enjoyment at home through the use of our products. We will leverage proprietary technology and state-of-the-art advancements to create products that consumers have not yet even dreamed of. We will make it happen.

This example provides a flavor for the type of future description that captures what you want your company to become. It helps to define what a company has the potential of becoming. It should also help to generate enthusiasm among employees, giving them an image of the future that each can be proud of and believe in. It should serve as a rallying cry for those involved in making innovation happen. It should motivate and inspire.

The innovation vision is critical for setting the stage to develop an innovation mindset. It better enables employees to envision the end results of innovation. It should offer a way for them to see and feel the eventual contributions of innovation to the enhancement of the company. This innovation vision should be the first initiative undertaken by your management team when you hold the innovation summit described in Chapter 7.

The Innovation Blueprint

The innovation blueprint describes the role of new products or services relative to the company's overall growth objectives and strategic plan. It offers a rough outline of the goals a company wants innovation to achieve over the next five years, from a broad perspective.

The blueprint should be no more than one page long. Its primary purpose is to serve as a "management contract," that is, to set the terms of understanding to guide innovation. Its key components include the following:

1. The overall growth role for new products
2. The estimated five-year budget
3. The people requirements
4. The revenue target for new products to fill
5. The role innovation will play with other growth modes
6. Top management's expectations and the type of involvement and participation they will have in the innovation process

The innovation blueprint frames the future picture that innovation will paint. A sample of an innovation blueprint appears in **Exhibit 6.2.**

It's very difficult to develop an innovation blueprint unless you have a five-year strategic plan already developed. The parameters and expectations for innovation must relate to a company's overall strategic plan. Without one, you're just throwing some innovation darts at the wall and hoping that you'll hit a bull's-eye. The problem, though, is that without an agreed-upon strategic plan, there is no dart board, far less a bull's-eye. So corporate business strategy comes first. Assuming that it is in place, you can then begin to build an innovation mindset by designing the vision and blueprint.

2. Develop an Innovation Strategy

The innovation strategy is a management tool that provides further detail on the guidelines for innovation and embellishes the innovation blueprint. It describes how the innovation blueprint can be implemented. It serves as the game plan to guide innovation initiatives. The

Exhibit 6.2

Innovation Blueprint

Role: High New Growth

Internally developed new products are expected to represent 50 to 60 percent of new revenue growth; 20 percent to come from acquisitions, and 20 to 25 percent from existing business.

Revenue Target

Corporate growth targets are to generate $150 million in incremental revenues during the next four years.

The target for new product revenues is $90 million by the beginning of year five.

Budget

The new product development expense budget for the next two years will approximate $5 million for salaries, market research, prototype development, and market-testing costs.

Capital available for plant and equipment investments needed for new products cannot exceed $7.5 million.

Commercialization launch costs cannot exceed 40 percent of year two revenue projections per new product.

Human Resources Requirements by Year Two

New product director

Four new product managers

Two business analysts

One market researcher

Three laboratory technicians

(continued)

Exhibit 6.2 *(continued)*

Innovation Blueprint

Interface with Other Growth Modes

Acquisitions will be aimed at acquiring product lines that will support or be complementary to the thrust of internally developed new products.

Licensing agreements will be limited to personalities that can be used in concert with new products developed.

Top Management's Expectation/Involvement

By year three, top management expects at least ten new products launched, representing cumulative revenue potential of over $50 million within one to two years.

Management also expects a steady pipeline flow of new product concepts to be established by the end of the first year.

Top management will attend all monthly new product steering committee meetings and will approve/disapprove the new product strategy, all concepts prior to prototype development, and any capital expenditures over $100,000.

Source: Thomas D. Kuczmarski, *Managing New Products: The Power of Innovation.* Englewood Cliffs, N.J.: Prentice Hall, 1992.

innovation strategy provides a rudder to the blueprint, which enables managers to steer innovation through uncharted waters. The innovation strategy will help you determine the future requirements for success and the expectations to be reached from new products and services.

An innovation strategy should define the following:

- The financial growth gap that new products and services will try to fill during the next five years
- The financial objectives to be met through innovation efforts
- The strategic roles that new products and services will try to satisfy
- The screening criteria to be used for moving ideas and concepts through the development process

Without an innovation strategy, it becomes difficult to know in which direction to head. First, financial goals and screening criteria calibrate the relative size and quantitative performance expectations of new products and services. They help to separate out the "can do" from the "would like to do" new product concepts. Second, strategic roles link all innovation activities to the business strategy through the innovation blueprint. They provide the qualitative benchmarks to guide new products and services development.

To show you the components of an innovation strategy, I have selected the examples depicted in **Exhibits 6.3 and 6.4. Exhibit 6.3** shows the financial growth gap for a $500 million company that new products will be striving to fill. **Exhibit 6.4** presents two examples of strategic roles and screening criteria.

This up-front planning, thinking, and discussion about innovation helps to take the uncertainty out of what new products and services are striving to achieve. This plan provides new products participants with a clear understanding of what they are shooting for. While goal setting and planning for innovation take time, companies that do so enjoy far better results from their motivated new products teams.

Exhibit 6.3

Defining the New Products Revenue Growth Gap for a $500 Million Company

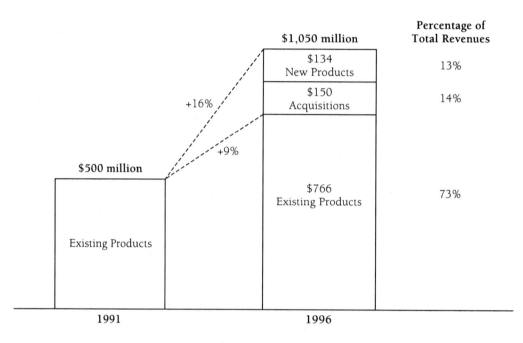

Source: Thomas D. Kuczmarski, *Managing New Products: The Power of Innovation.* Englewood Cliffs, N.J.: Prentice Hall, 1992.

The innovation strategy should be no more than a couple of pages. The objective is to simplify and clarify the expectations for innovation, not in any way to complicate them. The innovation vision, blueprint, and strategy have to be usable and readable. It's certainly a good idea to have large, poster-size enlargements of each of these hanging on the walls of the innovation department to give innovators a constant reminder of the map that should guide their activities.

Exhibit 6.4

Strategic Roles and Screening Criteria

$1 Billion Consumer Packaged Goods Company

Requisite	Opportunistic
• Secure dominant product share • Penetrate Canada • Enter mass-merchandiser channel • Increase shelf space exposure • Utilize waste by-product • Convert non-users of existing product	• Manufacture and market differentiated consumer product • Utilize off-season capacity; offset business cycles • Exploit existing technology in new way • Establish foothold in new geographic market • Utilize existing production capabilities

Common Criteria for All Roles

- Category growth at least comparable to inflation rate
- Fragmented competitive market with few national consumer packaged goods manufacturers
- Utilizes similar distribution/transportation network
- No high-technology component

• Premium-priced, high margin, value-added differentiated consumer product • Distributed primarily through grocery trade • Raw material related to product • Production process similar to product • New product shelf-life four to six months • Minimal coverage of competitive product by existing broker force • Gross margin must exceed 35–40%	• Regionally oriented business • Product with differentiated value-added or cost-competitive potential • Gross margins must exceed 40–45%

$300 Million Durables Company

		Qualitative Screens	Quantitative Screens (by year 3 after launch)
Strategic Roles	Preempt competition and defend share:	Must generate at least a 2% market share increase.	20% ROIC
	Expand into foreign market:	Affords the fomation of a new consumer business.	25% ROIC
	Utilize waste by-product:	Must be distributed via existing channels.	12% ROIC
New-Product Types	New-to-the-world:	Must utilize in-house technology patent.	$5 million sales; 40% gross profit margin
	New-to-the-company:	Competition must be fragmented; no new competitors with over a 70% share.	$3 million sales; 35% gross profit margin
	Line extensions:	Must be perceived by consumers as better than competitors' offerings.	$.5 million sales; 25% gross profit

3. Design a Technology and Innovation Portfolio

Aligned to each strategic role should be an identification of the core technologies or technical expertise areas that you anticipate will be necessary for developing new products. The first step is to inventory the current technologies that are still in a research exploration phase. For example, at 3M, the company undergoes an evaluation of its core technologies annually. Developing a technology portfolio prevents one from trying to match a technology with a new product idea. Rather, you're trying to identify a core technology as a launching pad for a variety of potential new products. Alternatively, core technologies might be one ingredient in the formation of an innovative new product.

For example, if a core technology at 3M is micro-encapsulation, this know-how can be applied to a broad spectrum of potential new products. The technology portfolio should help to define how a company will capitalize on technology to gain competitive advantage protection. Critical to the successful alignment of core technologies to strategic roles is the need to determine which technologies you plan to further fund and why. Core technologies should define the technological skills or scientific arenas that are in some way controlled by your company. It's fine to have strategic technological ventures or alliances with other constituencies, but the key is to have exclusive access to these technologies in certain applications or in specified markets.

Core technologies provide competitive advantage protection and can offer some defensive ammunition to a new product—to give it at least a few extra months of uniqueness before competition tries to copy it. Once core technologies and new technical skill areas have been identified for innovation efforts, adequate investments and appropriate technical talent must be secured. The challenge is to accurately identify the technologies that can best be exploited and provide competitive strength to the new products under development.

4. Design a Staged Development Process

A staged development process will provide your new products and innovation teams with a structure to guide them as they transform a new idea into a living, breathing, new product. The purpose of a staged process is to:

1. Provide a logical approach for systematically creating something new
2. Enable decision and approval points to be integrated into the process after each stage
3. Offer a way to manage this process by tracking the number of new concepts under development at any one time in each stage

A good way to understand how this works is to start at the final stage, commercialization. Let's assume you're expecting two successful new products to be launched in a given year. If you achieve a 50 percent success rate, this means you'll have to launch four new products into the marketplace. If we continue to back up from there, we might then need to have six to eight products in test market, eight to ten developed concepts that will come out of the business analysis stage, 15 to 20 in the concept development stage, and 25 to 30 new ideas in the up-front stage.

The value of this step-function progression is that it enables you to measure what's in the "hopper" at each stage. This pipeline flow helps you to project how many new products can be expected to be launched and by when. (See **Exhibit 6.5.**) Each stage of the process is defined as follows:

- **Consumer Problems and Needs Exploration:** Conduct qualitative research with consumers to explore and identify their gripes, complaints, hassles, and problems that they experience in a given product category, activity, behavior, or function. These problem areas provide a focus for idea generation.

- **Problem Solving and Idea Generation:** Generate new solutions and creative approaches that address the identified consumer problems. An idea is a description of a product that details what a product does and lists the key benefits that will be provided to consumers.

- **Concept Development:** Take screened ideas and develop them into "three-dimensional" descriptions of a product. A concept should describe the product features and attributes, its intended use, and its primary benefits to be perceived by consumers. It outlines the core technologies that will be used and states general technical feasibility. It addresses how the product might be positioned against competition and defines who the primary purchaser will be.

- **Business Analysis:** Formulate a market and competitive assessment that projects the potential revenue size and attractiveness of the new product concept. Develop a rough, three-year pro forma that estimates future financial performance.

- **Prototype Development:** Complete development of the product and run product-performance and consumer-acceptance tests.

- **Plant Scale-Up:** Determine roll-out equipment needs and manufacture the product in large enough quantities to identify "bugs" and problems. Run additional product-performance and quality tests.

- **Market Testing:** Launch the product into select test markets to gauge potential performance and educate target buyers.

- **Commercialization:** Introduce the product and sell it to the trade. Initiate awareness building and trial stimulation programs to reach the targeted consumer base.

- **Post-Launch Checkup:** Monitor performance of the new product at six and twelve months after launch and evaluate potential changes or improvements to be made.

Exhibit 6.5

Staged Innovation Development Process

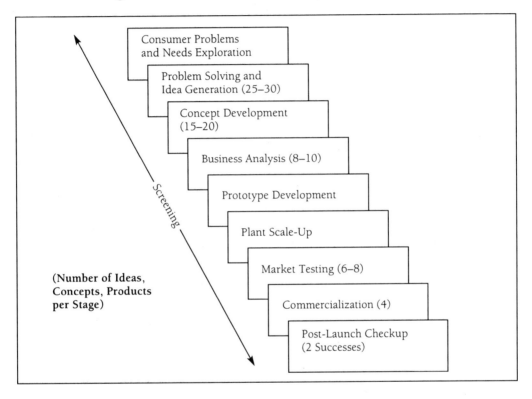

Consumer Problems and Needs Exploration

Problem Solving and Idea Generation (25–30)

Concept Development (15–20)

Business Analysis (8–10)

Prototype Development

Plant Scale-Up

Market Testing (6–8)

Commercialization (4)

Post-Launch Checkup (2 Successes)

Screening

(Number of Ideas, Concepts, Products per Stage)

In effect, this staged process enables a team to answer the following questions during the development life of a new product:

1. What might we offer?
2. Can we make it work?
3. What results can we expect?
4. Are we on track and ready to go?
5. How are we doing and what have we learned?

You can also think about this process of creating a new product as similar to the birth of a child. The consumer problem exploration stage is the innovation foreplay, the idea generation stage is the innovation conception, the concept development stage is innovation gestation, and commercialization is innovation birth. At your innovation summit, you should customize these process stages to suit the specific needs of your company.

5. Form Innovation Teams

The formation of innovation teams is a critical building block for effective innovation. Simply put, you just can't do it without them. This step is absolutely essential for ensuring that innovation will happen efficiently and effectively. Ultimate success lies in the hands of these teams. The productivity and performance of these teams will make or break innovation. Take enough time to figure out the right mix of team members, the appropriate team leader, and the skills required from different functional areas to get the job done. Forming, motivating, leading, and rewarding these teams will be tantamount to success.

There are four key components to an ideal new products or innovation team:

1. Cross-functional representation
2. Full-time, dedicated team leaders
3. Rewards that recognize performance
4. Regularly scheduled meetings

Cross-Functional Teams

Team members should represent a mix of different functional areas to provide a cross-section of expertise, perspective, and experience. No one functional area is more important than another. The selection of functional representation depends on the type of company and the industry in which it competes. The most common functional areas to choose from include sales, marketing, R&D, engineering, finance, manufacturing, market research, information systems, and customer service. On average, the most effective teams will have five to seven members.

Each member of the cross-functional team should have a stake in the project team. They need to share a common commitment to the team. This does not mean that team members are just assigned to teams. They must want to be part of an innovation team. At times you'll need to "sell" an individual team member on the merits of joining an innovation team, but it's essential that team members quickly get on board and develop a desire to participate.

Of utmost importance is the need to gain support for these innovation teams from functional management. It's essential to ensure that innovation team members are not penalized by their functional bosses for participating in innovation. Each team member must have some portion of his or her functional responsibilities reduced to provide time for working on the innovation team. There is nothing worse than just adding on responsibilities and increased time commitments without reducing the functional work load. So spend some time discussing team member candidates with their functional managers to ensure they support the endeavor.

Selecting the right cross-functional team members is also important. Don't just take people who are available or relatively inexperienced, whom functional managers wouldn't mind giving up. Instead, go for the best. Try to determine the mix of individuals that will bring "best of breed" to each innovation team. The ideal is to secure team members who bring a mix of creativity and analytical problem-solving skills.

You need to find people who have an in-depth interest, with personal motivation already high. In general, they should be strong team players with positive, proactive, and effective people skills. You need people who can work well independently but are strong team players as well. What's one word that captures the essence of the characteristics of the type of people most highly desired? A Renaissance person.

A Renaissance person has broad, multifaceted skills, is good at juggling multiple projects and people, is sensitive to others' needs, is an active listener, and is able to work well with others in a team setting. Again, his or her own personal motivation for participation must be high. Don't try to force-fit a member to a team. It will cause far more damage to the team dynamics than it could possibly be worth. In short, identify the top candidates for each innovation team, determine their interest level, clear their participation with their functional managers, and form the teams.

The amount of time each member allocates to the team will vary somewhat by project. However, a model to use in allocating time commitments for team members follows:

- Team leader: Full-time, 100 percent involvement
- 1–2 team members: Full-time, 100 percent involvement
- 3–5 team members: 30–50 percent involvement

It's important to have at least one team member besides the team leader who spends 100 percent of his or her time on this team. It's fine for other members to spend only one-third to one-half of their time on the team, but don't go below a 30 percent time commitment. Anything less than that turns into a "face time" form of participation. A cameo appearance on an innovation team just doesn't work.

Full-Time, Dedicated Team Leader

The starting point for creating innovation teams is to secure the right team leader. The background and previous experience of the individual is far less important than are his or her skills in motivation, communications, problem solving, and association making. Each should be creative, show initiative, and have team-building and conflict-resolution acumen and experience. These attributes separate the winners from the losers. In order to take advantage of the collective experiences, insights, and capabilities of team members, team leaders must have the ability to motivate people to realize their potential and to excite people about contributing to the team.

Team leaders need to be willing to get their hands dirty, and not just "manage" the team. The team leader is the one person who is ultimately accountable for the effective management and coordination of the team, and also for the new product results generated by the group. However, this accountability should be shared with the group and obviously cannot be conveyed in an autocratic manner.

Team leaders should be high achievers who possess many of the same characteristics cited for team members. The big difference for the team leader, however, is that this person must be a strong motivator, team builder, cultivator, and coach for the team. The leader, in effect, becomes the team sponsor. This person should have demonstrated people skills and experience in working effectively with various functional departments.

The team leader is responsible for energizing the team. As depicted in **Exhibit 6.6,** he or she should ask all team members to articulate their own personal objectives and goals for wanting to be on the team. It's also a good idea to talk about team member fears, concerns, and challenges regarding team participation and individual roles on the team.

At the team kick-off, the team should establish a shared set of norms and values, which will be discussed more in the eighth building block. The team leader should provide team members with continuous, positive feedback, offer team financial rewards, motivate team members, and establish a common innovation language that cross-functional team members understand and use. The team leader will also need to define the level of autonomy the team has and articulate which decisions can be made by the team without senior management. Beyond doing the work and getting successful new products launched, the team leader will spend a good deal of time energizing the team.

Exhibit 6.6

Energizing Innovation Teams

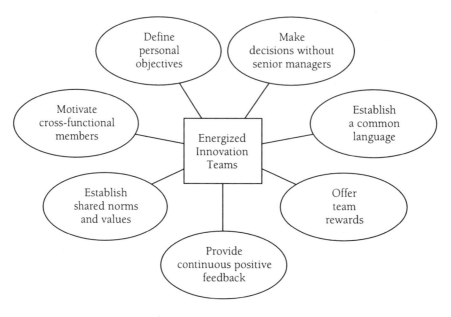

Rewards That Recognize Performance

Financial and non-financial rewards that recognize performance are critical for effective innovation teams. Make the team contributions count. Reward team members with financial cash bonuses, stock options, etc. Individual and team financial rewards are the glue that can join a team together and provide the added boost of high octane to fuel their motivation.

Rewards come in different shapes and sizes. Effective rewards are more than just coins and dollar bills. Often, the non-financial forms of recognition bring significant motivating power to team members. As shown in **Exhibit 6.7**, in Kuczmarski & Associates' 1993 survey, the number-one motivator cited by team members was a sense of personal accomplishment. This attribute is one that each team leader should be striving to help all team members achieve. People want to feel good about what they do. They want to know their contributions are adding value to the team. They want to feel that they have accomplished something intrinsically worthwhile.

According to new products team members, other valued non-financial rewards include peer recognition, top management exposure, and career advancement. Senior management needs to acknowledge these factors and provide opportunities to make them available. Company-wide innovation awards, other group-recognized rewards, access to senior management, career-pathing, and promotions should be part of the reward system.

Exhibit 6.7

Team Member Motivational Factors

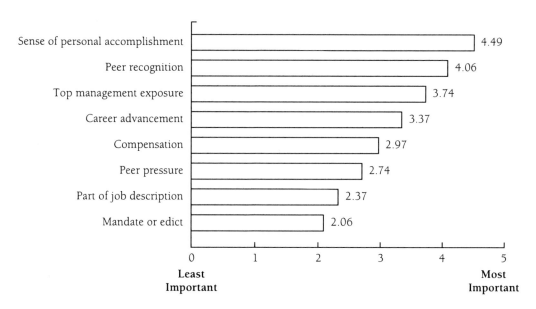

Source: "Winning New Product and Service Practices for the 1990s," Kuczmarski & Associates, Inc., 1993.

Regularly Scheduled Meetings

Team leaders can serve as the linchpin for marshaling the collective talents of a team to achieve successful innovation results. Teamwork requires effective leaders who foster open and candid communications. Innovation is not a process that allows team members to hibernate in their cubicles for weeks at a time. Weekly dialogue, at a minimum, is a must for all team members. Regularly scheduled meetings each week accomplish four things:

1. They provide a forum of communication to update each team member on progress being made, insights being uncovered, and new ideas being generated.
2. They enable conflicts or issues that may surface among team members to be resolved.
3. They provide a mechanism to keep the team on track and moving forward.
4. Probably most importantly, they provide a platform for other team members to share thoughts, analysis, and new thinking.

Innovation cannot be done in isolation. There is great benefit in sharing ideas and sparking additional thoughts among team members.

There should be a mix of meeting types. There is great value in having a regularly scheduled team meeting for four hours on the same day each week, but other types of meetings also warrant attention. These include dinner, breakfast, and lunch meetings; a full-day, off-site meeting; and a two-day workshop meeting. Different settings will foster greater relationship building and often help to stimulate greater creativity.

These regularly scheduled meetings should occasionally be held off-site so that informal relationships can be further built with team members. If each team member knows and understands the values, objectives, underlying motivators, and personality characteristics of other team members, greater collaboration and team effectiveness will result.

For innovation teams to be effective, management should spell out potential career paths for full-time team members. Each participant must have some idea of what's in store for him or her after the team has completed its goals. Often, an innovation team exists for one year or longer. Consequently, team members need to know how and when they will be transitioned back to their previous functional area. Alternatively, a career path can be created for them in innovation. Making a career path in the innovation area is best, because it affords a clear-cut commitment to innovation as an integral business function of the company.

6. Establish Reward Systems

Establishing rewards and incentives based on performance can also have high impact on team member motivation and behavior. The key objective is to simulate the same type of risk/return situation that entrepreneurs encounter. This means that often a certain amount of one's own money is at risk. It also means that this investment might end up with zero return or, alternatively, generate a high upside return, with no ceiling placed on how high is up. But the major component of an entrepreneurial investment is that it usually evolves over a period of time. Yields are not generated overnight nor in the short term.

To stimulate innovation, you need to pay people according to the real-world market performances of products and services they develop and deliver. Each individual team member and the group as a whole should have the opportunity to be rewarded relative to their innovation success.

Exhibit 6.8 depicts financial reward structures currently in use and preferred by new products teams. A resounding desire for pay-on-performance is evident. Compared to the types of bonuses and performance-based rewards currently in place, new products team members show a high degree of preference for team and individual bonuses, performance bonuses, and making an investment that enables the team to share in the financial returns. This research suggests that many people involved in innovation would be more motivated by a new form of compensation than by the more common base salary and bonus with a relatively narrow range (10–20 percent of base).

An incentive system can be structured according to absolute dollars, a percentage of profits, or revenues generated from new products. It might include innovation "phantom stock" for all new products developed by an innovation team. The key is to tie some major portion of

Exhibit 6.8

Desired Financial Rewards for Innovators

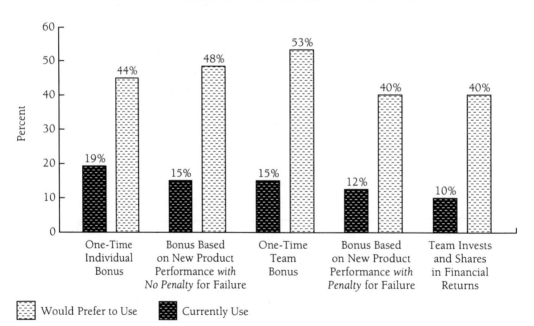

Source: "Winning New Product and Service Practices for the 1990s," Kuczmarski & Associates, Inc., 1993.

the compensation directly to actual market performance. Let's examine two potential pay-for-performance alternatives, phantom stock options and long-range team bonuses.

Innovation Phantom Stock Investment

Team members can buy phantom stock options on the new products portfolio they plan to develop. Up to 10 percent of the "stock" can be purchased. The "purchase" price might be set according to an estimate of new product development expenditures planned during the next year. If $800,000 is the "purchase" price, then a 2 percent ownership by a team member would cost this internal investor $16,000. If the new products launched generated $500,000 in new profits during the next five years, the team member (investor) would receive 2 percent of $2.5 million or $50,000. In contrast, if the new products launched end up as market failures, the total $16,000 up-front investment would be lost.

Long-Range Team Bonus

Team members would receive zero bonus in the first and second year, and in the third, fourth, and fifth year would be paid based on the actual performance of the new products they launch during the first two years. The bonus could be based on a percentage of total cumulative profits generated from the commercialized new products. The bonus payout should be sizable and meaningful to stimulate an entrepreneurial mindset. That is, paying each team member more than $100,000 in years 3, 4, and 5, assuming new product performance has been achieved, is totally appropriate.

Team members need to be rewarded for risk taking. Their paychecks should reflect the performance of the new innovations that they helped to create, without the standard ceilings, ranges, and bonus increase limitations.

As mentioned earlier, remember to develop a non-financial reward system, too. The more rewards the merrier, as long as each one is meaningful. As shown in **Exhibit 6.9**, new product team members want these types of rewards in concert with financial remuneration. "Pats on the back," notes, and positive comments recognizing good performance; increased job responsibility and budget authority; awards; and social interaction opportunities with senior management are all perceived as significant and valuable means of motivating innovation team members.

Combinations of both financial and non-financial rewards, when tied to performance, can help greatly to solidify an innovation mindset and build high-powered and high-performing innovation teams.

Exhibit 6.9

Desired Non-Financial Rewards for Innovators

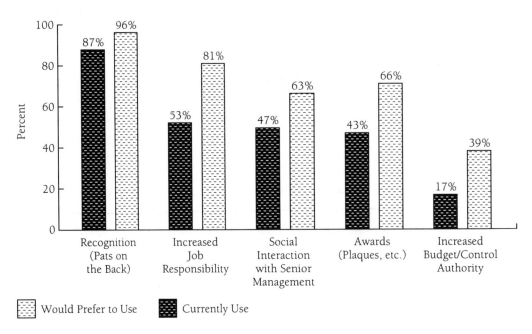

Source: "Winning New Product and Service Practices for the 1990s," Kuczmarski & Associates, 1993.

7. Measure Progress and Returns

Whatever gets measured and rewarded is almost always what employees will pay attention to. Job security and annual five percent base salary increases might work for many managers, but innovation players should be encouraged to go after products and services with radically new benefits with commensurate higher risk. Changing team members' compensation system to support this behavior is a critical component of creating an innovation mindset.

The starting point should be to determine the most important performance measures. Three categories of measures should be considered:

- **Company-wide** innovation measures, which describe how well the entire new products portfolio is performing, resource investment efforts, and resultant return on innovation

- **Team** innovation measures, which define how well the new products pipeline is being managed; that is, the number of concepts at each development stage, success rates, survival rates, budget variances, and the actual financial returns generated from the team's new product launches

- **Individual** innovation performance measures that evaluate a team member's contribution to the team's new product results

Specific innovation performance measures will be described in detail in Chapter 8. The relevant point is to evaluate and pay innovation participants according to expectations and tangible results. This might include the three-year financial results of one or more new products or a portfolio of new product types. It can be based on the number of new products that reach the test-market stage or the extent to which the team generates a balanced portfolio of new product types. The exact measures used will be tailored to your own company's innovation goals and stage of development. But there is one common return measure that should be used by all companies—return on innovation. The formula for measuring return on innovation follows:

$$\frac{\sum \text{Cumulative Net Profits Generated from New Products Launched}}{\left(\begin{array}{c} \text{Research} \\ \text{Costs} \end{array} + \begin{array}{c} \text{Development} \\ \text{Costs} \end{array} + \begin{array}{c} \text{Incremental} \\ \text{Production} \\ \text{Investments} \end{array} + \begin{array}{c} \text{Initial} \\ \text{Commercialization} \\ \text{Prelaunch Costs} \end{array} \right)}$$

The time frame for calculating return on innovation should be a three- to five-year period. For example, assume ten new products were launched during four years. Six new products generate a cumulative net profit of $50 million during that time. Four were failures. Allocated research and the new product development costs for ten new products was $12 million, incremental production investments were $10 million, and the prelaunch commercialization costs were $8 million for a total of $30 million. This yielded a return on innovation of 167 percent, or more than one-and-a-half times the total investment. Putting that $30 million in Treasury Bills would certainly have minimized the risk, but it would never have generated that attractive level of return.

The key point is to track your returns on innovation over time and measure the yields that have been generated from your innovation investments. In addition, take the time to create the performance benchmarks, measure progress against them, and pay innovation people relative to the outputs or satisfaction levels each one achieves.

8. Infuse Innovation Norms and Values

As Susan Smith Kuczmarski and I describe in our book *Values-Based Leadership,* values are shared goals, beliefs, ideals, and purposes of a group. Values often evoke inner convictions and emotional feelings among group members. In order for a group to maintain a set of values, the group must establish norms that shape and influence the ongoing behaviors, attitudes, and activities of its members. Values and norms help to solidify a team.

Norms, in turn, are based on the cited values and are the expected behaviors and style and form of communications adopted by a group. They are group-decided codes of conduct. A norm is a standard to guide group behavior. Norms involve shared expectations. They are the composite embodiment of group "agreements." Norms don't just happen, though. They emerge from what we propose as a three-step process:

1. There needs to be an expression of feelings, emotions, goals, motivators, and the like from each individual member of the group.
2. Individuals need to interpret and personally internalize them.
3. Through compromise and consensus building, each group member ultimately reaches agreement on the norms and values of the group.

If team members know what the group's goals, values, and norms are, they are motivated to work toward them without need for bureaucratic rules and regulations. Some companies have recognized the impact of establishing such a new products culture. W. L. Gore & Associates, which produces a wide range of products, including Gore-tex®, has four guiding principles to support its innovative culture:

- Try to be fair.
- Use your freedom to grow.
- Make your own commitments and keep them.
- Consult with other Associates prior to any action that may adversely affect the reputation or financial stability of the company.

As stated in an article by Frank Shipper and Charles C. Manz in *Organizational Dynamics* (Winter 1992):

This is a company without titles, hierarchy, or any of the conventional structures associated with enterprises of its size. Its management style is described as "unmanagement."

The primary benefits of this "un-structure" include direct lines of communication without any intermediary, no fixed authority, sponsors rather than bosses, and commitment to tasks and functions. By creating norms and values that emphasize the contributions of an entire team, a more effective organization can be created than one merely tied together through hierarchical reporting relationships.

As soon as innovation team members are pointed in the right direction through an agreed-upon set of norms, values, and clearly defined team goals, they will begin actively to achieve them. But each innovation team leader must nurture and cultivate the norms and values of the group. Drawing up a list of them at the first team meeting will not suffice. They need to be adopted, reinforced, and encouraged by team members. They provide the emotional glue to a team of cross-functional members who, very often, have not worked together before. Norms and values instill a sense of community, which can serve to get the group going.

Another good example of an innovation team with a strong set of values is the Saturn team at General Motors. The team set up a small car project and adopted a "clean-sheet" approach, vowing it would not be constrained by traditional thinking and industry practices. The team set itself up as a partnership and was described as follows in an *MIT Management* article by Richard G. LeFavve and Arnoldo C. Hax (1992):

The team enunciated five core values: commitment to customer enthusiasm, commitment to excel, teamwork, trust and respect for the individual, and continuous improvement.

The cornerstone of Saturn's leadership philosophy is that people want to be involved in making decisions that affect them. Their team construct was an extraordinarily effective one that embraced the key ingredients of team workmanship. These include shared leadership, team mission and purpose, individual and team accountability, and active problem solving as a group.

Developing innovation norms and values is imperative for each innovation team, but they are also important for your senior management team and other key functional leaders. In crafting a holistic innovation organization, you need to establish company-wide norms and values that encourage and foster innovation. You'll need to talk them up and then live by them. You'll need to take the company's pulse frequently to determine how well they are being lived up to on a daily basis. Innovation norms and values provide the threads to weave a successful innovation organization together. They're worth their weight in gold.

The eight building blocks provide the cornerstones for erecting a successful innovation program. You can't build an innovation mindset without all of them.

Innovation Checklist: The Eight Building Blocks

1. Create an innovation vision and blueprint.
2. Develop an innovation strategy.
3. Design a technology and innovation portfolio.
4. Design a staged development process.
5. Form innovation teams.
6. Establish reward systems.
7. Measure progress and returns.
8. Infuse innovation norms and values.

chapter seven

The Seven-Day Innovation Summit
Kick-Starting Your Organization

The present is a time of great entrepreneurial ferment, where old and staid institutions suddenly have to become very limber.

—Peter F. Drucker

Bill Gates, the founder and president of Microsoft Corporation, has been able to successfully maintain a high level of creativity and to instill an innovation mindset among his professionals. As described in an *Industry Week* article by DeAnne Rosenberg (August 17, 1992), Gates believes the key to innovation success is preserving excitement. He accomplishes this by holding regular retreats, encouraging 24-hour brainstorming via electronic mail and "schmoozing" among peers, and fostering fun and freedom among his employees. He makes sure that technical people are aware of innovation activities and makes them feel part of the corporate growth and innovation plan. He pays people based on performance and innovativeness, not based on tenure and title.

The principles used at Microsoft are appropriate ones to set the stage for an innovation summit. This should be a retreat—a retreat away from the daily "fire-fighting" and operating challenges. It should be a period of unencumbered and creative time. This chapter outlines the reasons to conduct a seven-day innovation summit, explains why the CEO should plan it, and provides the steps for designing a successful summit, including a suggested topic agenda.

Why not just hold a meeting around the boardroom conference table? What's wrong with a series of two-hour meetings spread out over a couple of months? Why should the CEO be at the center of the summit? The answer to these questions is momentum. To create an innovation mindset, you need to give your organization a kick-start. The innovation summit should be scheduled to last an entire week. The reason for this is two-fold:

1. There is enough innovation planning work and decision making to do that it will consume all of this time and then some.
2. You need an uninterrupted block of time with your management team to have a focused, concentrated, and motivating discussion about innovation.

You want innovation inertia to disappear. You want your management team to be totally immersed in innovation for a week. You want them to understand and believe in the importance of innovation to the future success of your company. You want them to know that you're committed to making it work.

The CEO at the Center

You might instinctively want to delegate the planning of the summit, but don't do it. This should be the CEO's meeting. It deserves one full week of your time and the focused attention of your management team. Don't talk yourself out of it. There will always be new crises, burning competitive issues, and urgent management challenges to deal with. Just put them on hold until you return to the office from the innovation summit. Tell your shareholders and employees that you'll be back in a week, and, when you return, your company will have an innovation plan that everyone can be proud of.

The reason why *you* should lead the innovation summit is simple. You are the ultimate leader of innovation for your company. You are also the most instrumental person within the organization for creating an innovation mindset. You need to convey your passion for and belief in innovation. You can't delegate that. You need to demonstrate it and mean it. By leading the summit, you are elevating the importance of innovation to your management team. Don't give this privilege to some other manager. Keep it for yourself. Your company's future and innovation success require it.

Think of yourself as your company's innovation personal trainer. After years of not "working out" on a regular basis, innovation flab has set in. Your goal is to pump up your management team, strengthen their innovation muscle, and tone up your company's innovation body. You will have to be an effective coach and embrace a combination of discipline and a "you-can-do-it" motivational attitude.

If you leave the summit having convinced your management team that they truly have the power to increase the efficiency and effectiveness of innovation, you'll have six, ten, or twelve additional "apostles" to spread the innovation gospel to others within your company. If any of your key managers tends to be negative toward innovation, be sure to talk with them before the summit. Explain to them why they need to adopt a proactive and upbeat attitude for this meeting. An innovation mindset will get caught in the muck if participants spend the week building evidence *against* innovation.

At this point, you are probably wondering how a CEO can afford to take a week out of his or her busy schedule. Yes, it will be a time burden for the entire management team. But go back and take another look at your five-year strategic plan. You'll probably see some rather huge financial numbers that are expected to be generated from future new products and services. The magnitude of this financial gap should convince you that a week's time is well worth the investment. If innovation is integral to your company's future success, it will drive your shareholders' and employees' satisfaction and increase your own peace of mind, so just find the time. In seven days, God created the world. All I'm asking you to do in a week is to begin to create an innovation mindset for your company.

The Importance of Location

The summit should happen off-site—outside of the office. Pick a location that allows you and your management team to also enjoy some sun, skiing, sailing, or surfing. Choose a site that offers a bit of fun and allows team building to occur. The atmosphere of an outdoor environment often fosters more personal interaction and more effective communication among participants. The old behavioral patterns and ritualistic norms for meetings with the CEO should be left back at the office.

The critical objective for picking a site outside of the office is to set up the mindset that this meeting will be different from all the other management get-togethers. It signifies that innovation practices are going to change. The summit itself becomes a symbol for innovation's new beginning. Innovation won't be done the way the organization might remember it. By placing your management team in a new physical location, you send a message that you want innovation to take on greater importance and stature within the company.

Planning the Summit

The summit can't be totally regimented. You need to have some flex time in the schedule. Just getting out of your office and into other surroundings goes a long way toward keeping one's mind open to new ideas and new ways of doing things. So don't compromise on the off-site location approach.

Involving Senior Managers

Once the location has been set, you'll need to have several managers do some homework prior to the meeting. Have them gather some historical information on past new product and innovation performance. This will enable the team to better gauge new product efforts in the future. Ask them to conduct a mini-diagnostic on various benchmarks that will provide insights on the previous results of innovation. Choose at least a three-year or longer historical time frame.

Have them collect data on the financial revenues, profits, development costs, margins, elapsed development time, and forecast variances for each new product launched. Also, have them identify success rates, survival rates, and the overall financial performance of the entire new products portfolio during that time. See whether they can identify the strategic roles (even if they were never formally established) that each new product satisfied. Have them list the screening criteria used to evaluate new product ideas and concepts. They should also figure out the future financial gap that new products and services are intending to fill in the future. Have them try to determine the portfolio mix of past commercialized products by type (i.e., new-to-the-world, new-to-the-market, new-to-the-company, line extensions, new-and-improved, repositionings, etc.). Have them calculate the percentage of new product types for the entire portfolio.

The point of this homework is to have the summit participants do some thinking about past innovation performance and also to gather some relevant information for decision making at the meeting. So this preparation work should be viewed as both mind-setting and actionable. Each participant should be asked to prepare some of the homework. Don't leave anyone out of the assignments. You want them all to be a bit immersed in the topic prior to the summit.

Writing the Preparation Memo

Next, you should draft a planning and preparation memo to each summit member that discusses the reasons for the summit, gives the agenda, and lists a few questions to put participants in the appropriate frame of mind. This memo should be distributed at least one month in advance of the meeting to ensure each manager spends adequate time preparing thoughtful input.

Reasons for the Summit

The "reason for the summit" portion of the memo should describe in detail your views on the role of and need for innovation at your company. You should articulate your own personal conviction and commitment to enhancing and improving innovation effectiveness and efficiency. You should describe why you feel the duration of the summit is necessary, the results you hope to achieve, and a prologue of the innovation mindset that, with your management team's help, you want to create. You should describe the ultimate end output of the summit, which will be an innovation plan to guide the organization. You should convey passion and emotion in these messages.

Preparation Questions

Include some questions in your memo to set participants' frame of mind before the summit. Ask them to prepare answers, which can serve as excellent discussion starters at the meeting. Following are some examples:

- How would you describe the role of innovation in achieving our growth goals?
- What are your financial expectations for new products and services five years from now?
- Which stages of our innovation and new products development process needs the most help or improvement?

- What are the primary barriers or obstacles that exist today that impede successful innovation?

- What are your own personal goals and aspirations relative to innovation? What do you personally want to gain from your involvement with innovation?

- What do you think your role and mode of participation should be in the innovation process?

- What are your own fears and concerns regarding your involvement with innovation?

- Who are three people in our organization that you believe embody the characteristics of a successful innovation and new products leader? Why?

- How should we communicate the results of our innovation summit to the rest of the company upon our return?

You could ask your management team to jot down a written response to these questions prior to the summit and to give them to you. In this way, you can give some thought to their issues. You might also want to consolidate all of the responses by question and provide them to the group at the summit. One benefit of doing this is that managers will be able to see that their issues are probably not unique, but rather commonly shared by their peers. Be sure that you too respond to the questions. Your responses are probably the most important for setting the stage for a successful summit.

The Innovation Summit Agenda

A sample agenda for the innovation summit appears in **Exhibit 7.1.** Obviously, you will tailor the agenda to meet your own company-specific needs. You might already have some of these items in place, or you might want to spend more or less time on particular issues. But don't shortchange the seven-day commitment. Even if it looks as if it will only take four days to accomplish everything, spend the other three days getting to know your management team better, undertaking team-building activities, and exploring additional ways to accelerate innovation implementation with the rest of the organization. Day 7 on the agenda is critical. Unless you develop an action plan that describes how you plan to communicate the results of the summit to the rest of your organization, you'll dilute the power of the whole endeavor. EX 7.1

Exhibit 7.1

Proposed Innovation Summit Agenda

- **Day 1**: Develop an innovation vision and blueprint.

- **Day 2**: Create an innovation strategy and technology portfolio plan.

- **Day 3**: Design an innovation development process, including decision points.

- **Day 4**: Identify people resource requirements and potential new products team leaders and team members.

- **Day 5**: Define rewards, compensation, and measurement approaches.

- **Day 6**: Establish innovation norms and values to guide communications and behaviors.

- **Day 7**: Plan the "new innovation mindset" communications plan and roll-out approach to the organization.

Each of these agenda items matches fairly closely with the eight building blocks of innovation, which were described in Chapter 6. Refer back to those when developing a more detailed agenda. Be sure to identify the decisions to be made as well as the written outputs to be completed by the end of each day. Your goal should be to leave the summit with a preliminary innovation plan. It should enable you and your management team to return back to the office and begin to activate an innovation mindset at 8:00 A.M. on Monday morning. You will continue to revise and modify the plan after the summit, but the key is to start doing something with it as soon as you return. Don't keep it in the file cabinet.

Conducting the Innovation Summit

You should establish one operating norm at the outset of the innovation summit: All discussions during the week must be proactive, positive, and purposeful. You should convey that there is a lot to accomplish, many decisions to be made, and several outputs to be crafted. Consequently, there just isn't time for "side-bars," negative attitudes, or demoralizing diatribes. The group will represent the innovation desires of the organization. This meeting can't be the usual; it has to be different if an innovation mindset is to germinate.

It's a good idea to assign discussion leaders ahead of time to facilitate group conversation on each topic area. Make sure to have assigned roles, clear-cut decisions to make, and action steps to take at the end of each day's session. This will help bring the discussion to closure, summarize key decisions, and finalize the written outputs from each daily discussion. It's imperative that you complete the agenda for each day before moving on to the next day's agenda topic. There is a sequential topic flow to the proposed agenda. You start at the top with the wide-angled innovation vision and blueprint and gradually move toward the tactics and details of the innovation plan.

Written Outputs

The end written outputs should be approximately 12 pages. Keep it simple and be sure to get down the key points. More descriptive matter can be developed and communicated in more detail later, as each component of the plan is further enhanced. To help you envision the end outputs of each day's discussion, a sample of the topics to be addressed in an innovation plan is shown in **Exhibit 7.2.**

Commemorating the Summit

Consider concluding the summit with a ceremony in which you present a personalized gift to each participant that signifies your appreciation for his or her time, energy, and vision in developing the innovation plan. Each participant deserves a customized gift just for him or her. Don't give out the standard, universal plaques or coffee mugs. Make each gift unique, special, and tailored to the individual. Buy the gifts at Tiffany's—not at Kmart.

After the Innovation Summit

There are several ways to communicate back to your company the results of the innovation summit. One effective method is to schedule a series of two-hour meetings with small groups of ten to twelve employees to summarize the key outputs of the meeting. It's important, though, to try to reach as many employees as possible. If you share the results only with other senior managers, you'll set up an "us versus them" mindset, which will defeat the whole purpose of the summit. So make sure that, at a minimum, a representative sample of all employee types and levels is in attendance at these meetings.

This initiative can then be augmented by developing and distributing a CEO video on the "Future Vision for Innovation," as well as

Exhibit 7.2

Innovation Plan

Description of the innovation vision	The innovation blueprint, covering broad goals and expectations	The innovation strategy, including: • Goals • Strategic roles • Screening criteria	The technology portfolio plan and technical areas of expertise
Page 1	Page 2	Page 3	Page 4
A staged innovation development process, including key decision points	An assessment of people resources required to activate the innovation strategy	A list of potential innovation leaders and new product team members	A description of the compensation system for innovation participants
Page 5	Page 6	Page 7	Page 8
A compendium of the rewards to use to motivate innovation teams	The criteria and measurement approach for evaluating innovation effectiveness	An initial set of innovation norms and values	The "new innovation mindset" communications and action plan
Page 9	Page 10	Page 11	Page 12

through a two-page letter to all employees describing the highlights of the innovation summit. You can write an article about it in the company newsletter or in any other communication vehicle that has widespread distribution.

Strive to keep the innovation summit alive and well for many months into the future. You'll need to revisit many of the topics again at senior management staff meetings. You might want to hold a two-hour meeting update each quarter to monitor progress made on the innovation plan. As I'll discuss in the next chapter, you will need to form a shared leadership innovation team and activate several organizational and communications changes. You'll want to ensure that innovation gets the level of management support and emotional hype that it warrants. Keeping your foot on the innovation accelerator pedal will provide the momentum needed to propel an innovation mindset.

Within a year, you should notice some major changes in the way in which innovation is practiced at your company. However, it will probably take at least a year, so don't become impatient or discouraged along the way. Maintain your conviction for innovation. To conclude, let me share with you an example of a company that has successfully cultivated an innovation mindset—Honda.

During the past two decades, Honda has transformed itself from a small and struggling domestic motorbike company to a global manufacturer of a diversified product line including autos, motorcycles, lawn mowers, and power-generating equipment. They attribute their success to constant and continuous innovation. Management demands that its new products satisfy high quality and performance standards. They utilize and leverage breakthrough technologies as a way to differentiate their new products to provide consumers with new benefits.

Honda fosters an open environment in which all employees are encouraged to express their opinions with no fear of retribution by some higher-up manager. The company fosters innovative thinking and enjoys a resultant flood of new product ideas, which come from all levels up and down the organization. They inform their employees about innovation goals, and they consistently demonstrate that Honda is committed to and values innovation. Their success has not been accidental. It has come through a fervent belief in innovation.

The innovation summit can be the opening scene for creating an innovation mindset. By involving your management team in the innovation plan, you will secure much greater commitment and buy-in from them for helping you to shape an innovative company. Now all you need is to get down to business and make it happen. Remember, you are the innovation leader. Its success is up to you, but you can't do it alone. Chapter 8 discusses some organizational considerations to help you implement the innovation plan.

Innovation Checklist: The Seven-Day Summit

1. Block out a week when key players are available.
2. Select a site conducive to team building and new thought patterns.
3. Involve senior managers in gathering information.
4. Draft a planning and preparation memo including questions to set participants' frame of mind.
5. Write the summit agenda.
6. Set ground rules on the first day of the summit.
7. Complete each day's agenda items before moving to the next.
8. Coordinate and communicate the written outputs of the summit.
9. Follow up on the summit by keeping innovation top-of-mind for all participants.

chapter eight

From Mindset to Results
Building Your Team and Measuring Innovation Progress

A non-creative environment is one that constantly bombards us, I said, overloads our switchboards with noise, with agitation and with visual stimuli. Once we can detach ourselves from all these distractions, find a way of "inscape" or "centering," the same environment becomes creative again.

—Frederick Franck, *The Zen of Seeing*

Having returned from an energizing and inspiring innovation summit, you sit down and begin to jot down some of the near-term action steps for implementing the innovation plan. You soon become overwhelmed and a bit frustrated. Some self-doubt creeps in about whether your organization can really pull this off. You fully realize that you cannot lead this innovation effort alone. You're afraid that your management team has already forgotten a good deal of what was discussed at the summit. You fear they have lost their conviction for innovation. You even begin to doubt yourself.

All of these reactions are natural. The magnitude of effort required to create an innovation mindset is formidable. It will be challenging. But don't be discouraged. You can most decidedly pull this off and achieve success. Remember, you are the innovation coach and leader who has the authority and expertise to make people understand the value of innovation for your company's future growth and long-term survival. But because of the complexity and sheer difficulty of managing innovation on an ongoing basis, you'll need to develop a shared leadership team to assist you with the tasks of innovation.

The Shared Leadership Team

Establishing a shared leadership innovation team is the best way to implement your innovation strategy and ensure that an innovation mindset is maintained and perpetuated. One of the best ways to convert this group into an effective, ongoing learning unit is to have each team member stay close to customers, suppliers, channel members, and other outside constituencies. Some successful innovation companies require their senior managers to spend, on average, one full day each month attending consumer focus groups or other consumer research endeavors. Others require field visits with sales reps to actually call on buyers at key accounts. One powerful approach is to schedule "top-to-top" meetings annually with your top ten customers. By listening to their needs, issues, and strategic considerations, you become better tuned into potential problems that innovation could resolve.

There are four organizational entities that comprise the shared leadership innovation team:

- A chief innovation officer or long-term executive officer (LEO)
- A vice president of innovation
- Innovation team leaders and their teams
- The senior management executive group

These four entities will join forces with you to work on instilling an innovation mindset throughout the organization. They will serve as the ambassadors and spokespersons of innovation. They, too, become coaches and sponsors of innovation. They represent the collective innovation team. With you at the helm, the group should steer the innovation ship to its planned destination.

Depending on the number of team leaders and members of your senior management team, the group should be no more than about 20 people. You need a group that is small enough that you could meet with most of them on a fairly regular and timely basis. View this group as your "Board of Innovation." In concert with you, the team holds the accountability, resources, and decision-making authority to make innovation work effectively. In fact, you should meet with the team at least one day each quarter. That's four meetings a year, which should fit into busy schedules if planned for at the beginning of each year.

If we count heads, and assume five innovation team leaders, a seven-person senior management executive group, one chief innovation officer, and one vice president of innovation, the total membership of this team would be 15, including the CEO. At the outset, it can be even smaller if you start with only one or two innovation team leaders. The essential message that you'll need to convey to this group is your desire for them all to adopt a shared leadership approach to innovation. This won't be easy at first, especially if they are used to a bureaucratic management style. But each member of this "board" needs to be a leader.

Each person needs to understand his or her role in the innovation process, believe in it, and have a high desire-intensity to make innovation a success. In order to perpetuate an innovation mindset and cultivate an effective shared leadership innovation team, you have to be willing to be self-critical, self-evaluative, open, and vulnerable. Otherwise, you and others won't be able to learn from mistakes made and better leverage them into future approaches. Your organization must be totally enraptured with learning from within. That is, your innovation leadership team should embrace the idea that mistakes are healthy as long as people learn from them. They need to know that you want a learning organization that continues to improve itself over time.

The Long-Term Executive Officer

The first position you should try to fill is the chief innovation officer, or long-term executive officer (LEO). Beware—this is a totally new idea and a controversial organizational position. There are multiple benefits to establishing this post, so try to keep an open mind to the merits of having a person like this help you lead innovation and longer-term initiatives of the company.

You'll need to think of the LEO as your partner in every sense of the word. Partnership is appropriate, because the LEO won't report to you, but rather will be your equal. That's right. This person and you would form a two-person team at the top. If this is too radical for you, it's possible to consider this position as your direct report. But before you discard the partnership idea, consider the benefits of sharing innovation leadership with another person at the top.

First, let's look at the role of the LEO. The LEO would report to the board of directors in tandem with the CEO to form a joint CEO-LEO partnership. The CEO would continue to focus on corporate strategy, organizational leadership, operational achievement, financial growth, and innovation effectiveness. The role of the LEO would be to lead longer-term growth initiatives, in particular innovation, R&D, new product development, and perhaps market diversification and global expansion. In effect, this person would manage initiatives with a five-year or longer horizon. Shorter term initiatives would be the responsibility of the CEO.

The LEO would serve as the long-term continuity officer of the company, driving initiatives with five- to ten-year goals and objectives. He or she would be responsible for long-term R&D investments and innovation projects, which are expected to have long development cycles and a long-term payback.

The LEO would also lead market diversification or global expansion initiatives that are anticipated to take several years to complete. For example, the company develops the objective to enter India or substantially increase penetration in the Pacific Rim. This requires the development of a series of new product lines, the opening of foreign offices, securing a new on-site management team, integrating information systems in the new country operations, and the like. The roll-out plan for this type of global expansion endeavor could easily require five or more years to complete.

A market diversification example could be to enter a new distribution channel to expand the reach of existing products to a new customer base. A commercial ceiling tile manufacturer might want to expand into the do-it-yourself retail market. This would most likely include the development of product line revisions, repositionings, and line extensions. Moreover, the current "brown" boxes will need to be redesigned with four-color packaging to serve the retail market to attract consumers. A new sales force will need to be hired and trained. A new management team will have to be put in place to run the operations of this new business. The LEO would manage these issues.

The LEO would also be the primary sponsor for helping you create an innovation mindset throughout the company. The LEO can help to foster long-term, broader, and more innovative thinking on the part of key managers. This can also help to balance the short-term financial mindset that market realities call for with a CEO. This LEO has the luxury of longer timelines to adequately create new businesses, new markets, and totally new innovations.

The LEO's compensation would be heavily geared toward the long term. An LEO should sign a ten-year employment agreement. It's important to view a ten-year contract as an essential component for a successful LEO formula. The cornerstone for the whole concept of the LEO is based on a long-term, tenured position. Compensation would be lower in the first five years ($200,000–300,000) and then leap upward in years six through ten. In the later years, the LEO must have the upside opportunity to earn millions of dollars in bonus incentives, depending on the return on innovation achieved, financial performance from R&D and product development investments, and the market success of diversification or expansion initiatives.

But why should a CEO risk giving up power and authority to an LEO? What can LEOs do that effective CEOs couldn't handle themselves?

CEOs should not be expected to lead all innovation and long-term growth initiatives for the entire company by themselves. More and more companies and boards of directors are examining the possibility of splitting the post of chairman and chief executive officer. They wonder whether a retired CEO should remain active in management and whether a chief operating officer and chief executive officer should be working together in a partnership rather than the more commonly found hierarchy.

About 20 percent of major U.S. corporations now divide the posts of chairman and chief executive officer between two people, according to a 1992 survey of 322 chief executives by recruiters Korn/Ferry International. However, this figure is expected to increase substantially during the next five years. Many executives believe this split will reach upward of 50 percent in all major corporations. Big institutional shareholders, in particular, are pushing for a separation of power at the top. Shareholders recognize that one individual can't manage everything, including long-term innovation.

CEOs will need to check their egos at the door for a CEO-LEO partnership to work. You can't start with the assumption that the other person is not as capable as you are. Rather, you need to see the increased power that this team could bring to improve innovation effectiveness.

Most CEOs of *Fortune* 500 companies have, on average, a five- to seven-year tenure. Many are in and out of office in less than five years. You can't expect a company to keep a steady course when the navigator keeps changing. It takes time to understand an organization, where it's been and where it's trying to head. The LEO can gain this longer-term perspective, which will pay dividends to the company in more ways than one. The LEO can offer long-term stability, provide equilibrium, and become the rudder of the corporate innovation ship. The LEO can provide the stamina, endurance, and "staying power" needed to balance the impact of organization shifts, downsizing, management mobility, and corporate restructuring.

From an astrological perspective, the sign Leo symbolizes the characteristics of assertiveness, steadfastness, determination, and will-power—not a bad description for a corporate LEO. The ideal LEO should have built a solid experience base by effectively managing and leading teams and should have a strong functional background in marketing, R&D, innovation, business development, or line operating management. Of utmost importance is that an LEO has already demonstrated an ability to see beyond—to be visionary. However, the LEO must be a visionary who makes things happen and can convert a long-term vision into a reality.

Because innovation and long-term growth are valuable components of most corporate strategies, the addition of an LEO to the senior management team is a tangible action step toward enhancing an innovation mindset. Instituting the LEO position also becomes a most visible sign to the organization and to the financial community that the CEO and his or her company are truly committed to the benefits of long-term innovation.

Finally, if the title of LEO seems to be a bit "soft" for you, calling this position the chief innovation officer is a perfectly acceptable alternative.

Vice President of Innovation

The role of the vice president of innovation is to be accountable for, lead, and manage the company's innovation strategy and its implementation. This position should report directly to the CEO-LEO partnership, but the LEO would have a closer, more day-to-day working relationship with him or her. Reporting to the vice president of innovation would be all of the innovation team leaders. Depending on the scope of innovation activities and goals, the number of team leaders could range from 2–3 to as many as 15–20. These team leaders all have cross-functional teams focused solely on development of new products and new innovations. The vice president of innovation should also have access to resources in R&D and technology. Some of the key roles of this position follow:

- To allocate resources
- To serve as an internal "barriers-buster"
- To monitor the progress of the innovation teams
- To coach and counsel the innovation team leaders
- To track performance of all new products launched

This person should be measured against return on innovation, team leader effectiveness, and the degree to which the company's overall innovation goals, strategy, and portfolio have been satisfied. Again, this position should be occupied by the same person for a relatively long time, at least five to six years. Compensation should be based heavily on performance and actual results achieved. A vice president of innovation should be able to double a base of $200,000 with a performance bonus potential of roughly the same amount.

Innovation Team Leaders

As discussed in Chapter 6, the innovation team leaders are, in effect, the people that ensure the innovation job gets done. They're involved in doing it, as well as leading it, on a team-by-team basis. They are the crew that ensures the innovation ship is functioning properly. They provide the day-to-day leadership with cross-functional expertise for creating newness. Similarly, their compensation should also be based on results, with a very high upside bonus.

Senior Management Executive Group

It's very important to keep innovation top-of-mind with the senior management executive group. Make innovation a corporate initiative. Schedule innovation reviews each quarter with them. Manage their interest in innovation and keep them committed. Make them active participants in executing the innovation plan developed at the summit. Keep them up to speed. Bring up innovation issues at staff meetings with this group. Keep their innovation mindset alive. Their involvement should increase their buy-in, making it easier for them to let go of some of their key resources to work on innovation teams.

In summary, this is the group of people who can assist and support you with the implementation of the innovation plan. This "Board of Innovation" should, in concert with you, serve the shareholders, employees, and customers of the company. It's your job to build a shared leadership mindset to maximize the collective skills and talents of this innovative group.

Celebrate the Failures and Party!

Most CEOs give lip service to accepting commercialized failures. There's only one real way to demonstrate a commitment to risk taking and convey an acceptance of failure: Hold failure parties! That's right. Host an elaborate, fun-filled affair with all of the team participants who worked on the new product. In fact, handing out $1,000 bills to each team member is a nice way of acknowledging their risk taking and your continued support for their efforts.

Making innovation happen requires courage. Companies like Microsoft, 3M, Coca-Cola, and General Electric have created environments where risk taking, newness creation, and invention are part of the company mindset. However, this mindset is rather atypical for most

U.S. corporations. The reason is that most leaders at the top are unwilling to stick their necks out, stay courageous, and continue to pursue innovation.

Downsizing and cost-cutting have created in many organizations a reactionary and defensive management mindset. People are worried about keeping their jobs. They are concerned about the future of their careers. Why should they take risks that could result in a major failure? However, thousands of entrepreneurs and courageous leaders within companies do take risks every day. They recognize that there is great potential upside and there are long-term benefits in charting a course to explore innovation. By celebrating failures, you convey to your organization an acceptance that risk taking will yield a mix of successes and failures.

Creating and Monitoring Innovation Indices

You will want to develop a set of performance indices with the help of your LEO and vice president of innovation that can be used to measure progress along the innovation front. These indices should be used as a management tool—not as a club with which to bludgeon the innovation team. The key is to use them as benchmarks and indicators of innovation progress and ways to improve its effectiveness in the future. The indices should serve three purposes:

1. Provide a snapshot in time of how well the innovation effort is progressing

2. Help calibrate the appropriate allocation of people resources and financial investments

3. Offer a diagnostic tool that can be used to pinpoint potential problem areas that might need fixing or shoring up

There are ten quantitative innovation indices that should be analyzed, measured, and monitored annually. These can best be used comparatively, to show how each index is changing from one year to the next. The purpose of these indices is not to generate some cutesy innovation score, but rather to improve decision making. Each index is best utilized as a metric of performance, comparing one year to the next. Several of these indices have a three-year time horizon built into the formula, others are based on annual performance.

Reviewing the composite results of all of these indices should tell the organization where it stands and suggest areas that require additional focus or investment. For example, if the R&D innovation emphasis ratio has declined for two consecutive years, this might signal a needed shift in the allocation of R&D budgets away from existing product cost reductions and improvements to new products.

The LEO, vice president of innovation, and all innovation team leaders should be highly knowledgeable about all of these indices. Their primary purpose is to enable this group to monitor innovation progress, rather than to serve as a report card. Moreover, it's imperative that this group is actively involved in the creation of any innovation indices the company plans to track. The group needs to help shape their development, be committed to them, and measure them consistently.

These measures will also serve as a common language for people from a variety of functional backgrounds. They provide a rallying point and a set of common definitions to guide decision making. The indices chosen to be measured by the company should be customized and linked to the innovation goals and strategy. For example, if new innovations are expected to fill a huge revenue gap during the next five years, then the newness investment ratio should be higher than it was in previous years. The top ten innovation indices and their formula calculations are presented in **Exhibit 8.1.** A description of each one follows:

1. **Survival rate:** A measure of the harsh reality of market acceptance. Indicates how many commercialized new products

Exhibit 8.1

The Top Ten Innovation Indices

Innovation Index	*Formula Calculation*
1. Survival rate (3 Years)	Number of commercialized new products still on the market ÷ Total number of new products commercialized
2. Success or hit rate (3 Years)	Number of new products exceeding three-year original revenue forecasts ÷ Total number of new products commercialized
3. R&D innovation effectiveness ratio	Cumulative three-year gross profits from commercialized new products ÷ Cumulative three-year R&D expenditures allocated solely to new products
4. R&D innovation emphasis ratio	Cumulative three-year R&D expenditures allocated solely to new products ÷ Cumulative three-year R&D expenditures
5. Innovation sales ratio	Cumulative third-year annual revenues generated from commercialized new products ÷ Total annual revenues
6. Newness investment ratio	Cumulative three-year expenditures allocated to new-to-world or -country products ÷ Cumulative three-year new product total expenditures
7. Innovation portfolio mix	Percentage of new products (by number and revenues) commercialized by type • New-to-the-world, -country • Line extension • Repositioning • New-to-the-company • Product line improvements
8. Process pipeline flow	Number of new product concepts in each stage of the development process at year-end
9. Innovation revenues per employee	Total annual revenues from commercialized new products ÷ Total number of full-time equivalent employees devoted solely to innovation initiatives
10. Return on innovation	Cumulative three-year net profits from commercialized new products ÷ Cumulative three-year new product total expenditures (for all commercialized, failed, or killed new products)

are still on the shelf or in distribution after a three-year period. This index provides a bare-bones minimum look at how your new products are cutting it in the market.

2. **Success or hit rate:** A measure of how well commercialized new products are performing financially relative to the original revenue or profit forecast. This metric provides insights on two different fronts. First, it indicates the accuracy of the process for forecasting new product revenues or profits, a process that takes place in the business analysis and market testing stages. Second, it provides a clear measure of the financial revenue or profit performance of all commercialized new products. A hit rate of more than 50–60 percent is excellent.

3. **R&D innovation effectiveness ratio:** A measure that shows how much bang you're getting for your R&D buck. Of course, the measure does not provide a precise correlation because of the lag between R&D expenses and results. It is a good metric to use to judge whether you are spending enough in R&D and whether you are spending it wisely. It also shows whether R&D investments can successfully be converted into new products that yield a solid return in gross profits. The reason for tracking gross profits versus net profits is to avoid all the debate and usual "clutter" that is associated with sales and marketing costs. This way you can look more directly at the contribution from new products.

4. **R&D innovation emphasis ratio:** A measure that clearly indicates how much of your total R&D investment is being allocated toward the development of new products. Depending on your innovation strategy and the importance of new products to your overall growth goals, this ratio can be adjusted appropriately. Usually, at least 50–75 percent of total R&D expenditures are dedicated to innovation when it has a high level of importance.

5. **Innovation sales ratio:** This measure indicates the overall magnitude of your innovation efforts compared to the total company revenue size. If innovation is important to growth, this ratio will usually be 15–25 percent or more annually.

6. **Newness investment ratio:** A measure that indicates the level of investment being allocated to totally and radically new innovations. This metric should be examined in concert with the innovation portfolio mix.

7. **Innovation portfolio mix:** This measure gauges the percentage of and actual revenues coming from each type of new product commercialized. Usually 30–40 percent of new products are in the new-to-the-world and new-to-the-company categories if a truly balanced portfolio is to be maintained.

8. **Process pipeline flow:** A measure that provides a snapshot of how full the new product development pipeline is. It is based on your company's historical conversion factors in terms of how many concepts are typically needed to yield a commercialized new product. It gives you a fairly good way to project the number of future commercialized new products that your current pipeline will generate.

9. **Innovation revenues per employee:** This ratio should continue to increase over time as the experience base of the people doing innovation increases. This measure also provides insight about the effectiveness of additional resource allocations.

10. **Return on innovation:** This is the grand-daddy measurement that provides a holistic look at the total return generated in terms of cumulative net profits from all innovation investments. (See **Exhibit 8.2.**)

Let's assume that during a three-year period a company launches ten new products. Seven of those are still on the market and four have exceeded original revenue forecasts. This would yield a 70 percent survival rate and a 40 percent success rate. Revenues generated from

Exhibit 8.2

Return on Innovation Calculation

$$\text{ROI} = \frac{\Sigma \text{ (Cumulative Net Profits Generated from New Products Launched)}}{R\left(\begin{array}{c}\text{Research} \\ \text{Costs}\end{array}\right) + D\left(\begin{array}{c}\text{Development} \\ \text{Costs}\end{array}\right) + \text{IPI}\left(\begin{array}{c}\text{Incremental} \\ \text{Production} \\ \text{Investments}\end{array}\right) + \text{ICP}\left(\begin{array}{c}\text{Initial} \\ \text{Commercialization} \\ \text{Prelaunch Costs}\end{array}\right)}$$

Example

$$\text{ROI} = \frac{\$ 8 \text{ million}}{\$ 32 \text{ million}} = 25\%$$

- 8 new products launched over five-year period

- 4 new products were successful, generating on average:
    $20 million annual revenues
    $2 million annual operating profits ($8 million in total profits)

- Average costs per new product launched:
R	($.5 million each)	$ 4 million
D	($1.0 million each)	$ 8 million
IPI	($.5 million each)	$ 4 million
ICP	($2.0 million each)	$16 million
		$32 million Total Costs

these ten new products in year three were $50 million for cumulative revenues of $80 million during the three years. With a 60 percent gross profit margin and a 15 percent net profit margin, cumulative gross profits were $48 million and net profits were $12 million. Cumulative three-year R&D expenditures were $20 million, with $10 million earmarked for new products. Revenues this year were $250 million. Cumulative three-year new product total expenditures were $24 million. In this example, the year three innovation indices would be as follows:

1. Survival rate   7/10 = 70%

2. Success or hit rate   4/10 = 40%

3. R&D innovation effectiveness ratio $$\frac{\$12 \text{ million}}{\$10 \text{ million}} = 120\%$$

4. R&D innovation emphasis ratio $$\frac{\$10 \text{ million}}{\$20 \text{ million}} = 50\%$$

5. Innovation sales ratio $$\frac{\$50 \text{ million}}{\$250 \text{ million}} = 20\%$$

6. Newness investment ratio $$\frac{\$6 \text{ million}}{\$24 \text{ million}} = 25\%$$

7. Innovation portfolio mix

	Number/Revenues	
New-to-world	20%	40%
New-to-company	10	20
Line extensions	70	40

8. Process pipeline flow

	Number per Year
Ideas	90
Concepts	12
Prototypes	8
Market tested	5
Commercialized	3

9. Innovation revenues per employee $\dfrac{\$80 \text{ million}}{20 \text{ employees}} = \$4 \text{ million}$

10. Return on innovation $\dfrac{\$12 \text{ million}}{\$24 \text{ million}} = 50\%$

This set of innovation indices is not intended to be comprehensive or all-inclusive. The tools should be developed to fit the specific requirements of your company. View them as a starter kit for measuring the progress of your innovation effectiveness.

There are certainly many other appropriate criteria, ranging from cycle times, to the time it takes to develop a new product, to new product quality, to team effectiveness. Pick the innovation indices that are right for you and your company. Without some, it will be difficult to inculcate an innovation mindset.

Using these innovation indices to measure your progress will provide great assistance to your "Board of Innovation." Over time, they will serve to motivate your company and guide the development of an innovation mindset. Creating an innovation mindset is a formidable task. However, you can do it. Now, get to work.

Innovation Checklist: Managing and Measuring Progress

1. Establish a shared-leadership innovation team with the authority to implement your innovation strategy. Make the team accountable for innovation performance.

2. Ensure that team members keep track of the market pulse by communicating with customers and channel members.

3. Make sure team members understand their roles clearly and project high desire-intensity to others.

4. Schedule top-to-top meetings to get input from your key customers.

5. Establish a leadership position with accountability for long-term results, including innovation performance.

6. Create effective innovation indices.

7. Host failure parties to convey acceptance of failure and encourage risk taking.

8. Develop innovation indices and employ them to monitor and manage innovation efforts.

9. Measure Return on Innovation to gain an overall picture of the net profits generated from innovation investments.

10. Make the compensation of innovation team members reflect innovation performance.

A Personal Perspective on Innovation

At first people refuse to believe that a strange new thing can be done, and then they begin to hope it can be done, then they see it can be done—then it is done and all the world wonders why it was not done centuries ago.

—Frances Hodgson Burnett, *The Secret Garden*

Nearly two decades ago, when I was a new products manager at the Quaker Oats Company, I became involved with innovation. At that time, I thought that innovation was a process, a creative new idea, or the launch of a new concept to market. I had no idea what was required to make successful innovation happen. I knew that I was kept busy with a set of activities: brainstorming sessions, concept tests, in-house usage tests, Q-sorts, prototype development, and packaging copy. But I missed the whole point. Innovation isn't a set of activities or action steps; it's a mindset. It's a way of life!

As much as other managers tried to describe to me how new products were developed and how innovation occurred, I really didn't get it. The reason I never quite grasped how to do "it" successfully was that everyone focused on the process. The emphasis was on detailing activities and developing timelines that showed scores of little steps that a new idea would have to pass through to reach the market. Most of the books I read at that time depicted innovation as a dry and routinized process.

So, in effect, if one took a creative idea, turned it into a concept that passed some quantitative research test scores, developed some financial projections, worked effectively with R&D to create a prototype, conducted some manufacturing and market tests, and convinced the sales force that *this* new product would be a real winner, then you had it. A successful new product. A big-hit innovation.

Early Perspectives on Innovation

But it didn't seem to work that way. Nor, as I later discovered, does a process-driven approach to innovation work well at any company. Something was missing. The hardest part was that I really didn't even know how to determine what was missing. So I proceeded to manage several simultaneous activities, kept my nose to the grindstone, and worked on the development of what several years later became Chewy Granola Bars and Aunt Jemima Microwave Pancakes.

However, this experience enabled me to develop some early perspectives on innovation. I began forming my own points of view about innovation, which provided me with a career's worth of curiosity to expand on and find answers to the ingredients of innovation success.

Some of my early impressions regarding the "missing pieces" for successful innovation and problems associated with the development of new products included the following:

- **New products didn't seem connected to the marketing strategies of the existing businesses.** It felt like I had been sent away to the Island of Innovation. There was a list of new product projects to work on, but there was little strategy behind the goals new products were supposed to achieve, beyond securing incremental profits.

- **I didn't see what was in it for me.** I felt I shouldn't take risks or have a long-term view. I knew if I worked hard I'd keep my job and get an annual base salary increase and the predictable bonus. But there was a lot of perceived career risk associated with new products. The "game" was to make sure you didn't stay in new products for more than 2–3 years. New products had second-class citizenship. The big brands with big advertising budgets were where the action was. That's why you would pay your dues in the new products area for a while, survive there, and return to the mainstream existing businesses as soon as politically possible. From my vantage point, I perceived no extra rewards if I launched big-hit new products, so my natural tendency was to focus on lower risk (and lower return) line extensions and "me-too," "better-than" types of new products. Besides, the truly new-to-the-world products would take years to develop, and I'd be gone from new products before I'd be able to take any credit for initiating them.

- **Senior management didn't want any failures—only successes.** They said that they supported taking risks, but only if the risks taken yielded successful new products. Again, my perspective was further framed down to a small window of low-risk new products.

- **It felt much too unfocused to start the new product development process with "random" brainstorming and idea generation.** I'd lead brainstorming sessions that were described as very effective. I'd leave those sessions with a list of 200 ideas generated by internal employees and managers. Now what should I do? There was no consumer need aspect to these ideas, no strategic context. How was I now supposed to pick out a handful of ideas to move to concept development?

- **I had to continuously fight to keep resources, both funding and people.** Which area had its budgets cut first when the quarterly earnings report was less than expected? You guessed it—new products. Moreover, since most people just wanted to be able to "check off" new products as they proceeded up the career ladder, it was difficult to motivate new products team members. Besides, many of the multi-functional team members had other "full-time" jobs. Their participation on a new products team was only an ad-hoc, part-time endeavor. It was a sort of corporate extracurricular activity. So resources management was a real challenge.

I soon became confused and simultaneously frustrated with this amorphous thing called innovation. It was hard work, an emotional roller-coaster. You never knew if the product you were working on would end up a success or a failure. However, I was told to roll with the punches and "get some new products out the door." Few people provided me with any definitive solutions, and virtually no one offered me concrete answers or surefire approaches that would guarantee innovation success. A few years later, I left Quaker Oats and wished the newly appointed new products manager the best of luck.

However, for better or for worse, I remained fascinated with the topic of innovation. I kept believing that if companies could find an effective way to achieve successful innovation, it would be their most powerful source of growth. I watched acquisition fever take hold in many companies. I kept wondering why so many companies sought acquisitions rather than to develop new products. It seemed as if managers were enthralled with financial wheeling and dealing. They seemed less enthusiastic about putting in place an effective innovation organization that could yield new product dividends far out into the future. By the late 1980s, I watched many of these allegedly risk-free acquisitions be spun off, sold, or diversified. For some odd reason, these clear-cut failures were never referred to in this way, but rather called portfolio balancing and redeployment of assets.

In the late 1970s, when I joined Booz • Allen & Hamilton, the management consulting firm, I wanted to explore the topic of innovation, better understand its components, and ascertain whether there were some secrets to doing it more effectively. I remained intrigued with innovation. Why? Because it is a creative, stimulating, and exciting endeavor. It can be an exhilarating experience. I wanted to help companies create something that had never before existed. I wanted to invent and shape something new. I wanted to watch, guide, and mold its development. I wanted to gain a sense of accomplishment and great personal satisfaction.

Big Is Not Necessarily Better

I soon discovered that some companies *had* discovered the secret to successful innovation and that a few people *had* figured out how to do it effectively and enjoyably. In fact, one of the most important observations that I made when I began my career in consulting was that small companies, for the most part, seemed to be far more successful at innovation than large corporations.

This was counterintuitive. The large corporations had much fatter wallets, hundreds more people, significantly newer technology, and a much richer platter of core competencies—all the essential ingredients to support an effective innovation effort. Yet they tended to fumble the ball, lose interest in the innovation game, and ultimately end the season with some good calls but a losing team. Why? Was it just because these resources weren't managed well or marshaled in a way that would harness their collective energy? In part that was true. In contrast, small companies took a different approach to innovation.

What I discovered was that CEOs at many small companies were actively involved in new product development and matched their actions to their words. They consistently supported innovation; conveyed a passion, fervor, and belief in it; and communicated a buoyant, positive, and can-do attitude about it. They created within each of their companies an innovation mindset. That is, a pervasive attitude that encouraged employees to think differently, to think beyond the way things are done today.

Learning about Innovation Firsthand

I eventually convinced the partners at Booz • Allen & Hamilton to fund a research project to study best practices in new product development. I thoroughly immersed myself in this fascinating topic. This study, called "New Products Management for the 1980s," was based on the new product practices of more than 700 companies, which launched more than 13,000 new products during a five-year period.

I was able to apply several useful findings from this study to real-world situations. I then continued to consult for a wide range of companies and gained further insights on what works and doesn't work for fueling innovation. I was able to recommend some new approaches for companies to take. Enough time has passed to see that many worked (and many didn't).

In hindsight, there was one common characteristic among the winning innovation companies: Companies that were able to grab the innovation throttle and accelerate the speed of new products to market concurrently increased their success rate. The common characteristic was a can-do CEO who had been able to create a culture that inculcated, talked about, and supported an innovation mindset.

At the same time, I started teaching as an adjunct professor at Northwestern University's Kellogg Graduate School of Business one night each week. That continued for 11 years. Approximately 2,000 students later, I realized I had also gained several important insights from their perspectives on innovation. Most of my classes consisted of evening students who worked full time. They would frequently talk about the myriad of cultural impediments and demotivators that erode and curtail effective innovation. I was able to develop another set of data points on what it takes to do innovation well. Apparently, senior management was once again perceived as instrumental to success.

About 13 years ago, I once again learned, firsthand, an important lesson about innovation. The CEO needs to be committed, involved, and an active participant. No question about it. I'd left Booz • Allen & Hamilton with aspirations of starting several new businesses. And why not? I knew a lot about innovation. I did extensive research and made sure that my business concepts provided attractive solutions to real problems experienced by consumers, business customers, and others.

I started a chain of unique flower retail shops; opened a consulting business; tried to purchase a school; came very close to opening Tommy K's, an upscale nightclub; and started a partnership to launch a delivery gourmet lunch service called Gourmet Brown Bag. And I really did believe I could do it all. I was buoyant, positive, upbeat, and had passion. The flower chain failed. I was outbid by some developers for the school. "Other" constituencies prevented me from getting into the nightclub business. I never found the right kitchen location for the lunch delivery business. However, the consulting business was a decided success.

I now had my own set of personal statistics to compare against. I had launched two businesses and consequently achieved a 50 percent success rate (the consulting business continues but the flower shops don't). Three out of the five new ideas never made it to commercialization. They went through a systematic new product/service development process, but they were never launched. I learned two things from this experience:

1. Failure is endemic to innovation.
2. There is a finite capacity for how much innovation can be achieved in a short time.

Perhaps if I had staged those five business ideas over a five-year period, rather than within nine months, more of them would be up and running today. But I also had accumulated one more learning data point: CEOs can make or break successful innovation. I had tried to do too much.

During the past 13 years, I have consulted for nearly 100 companies while founding and building Kuczmarski & Associates, one of the top 100 management consulting firms in North America. I have remained fascinated with innovation and have accumulated additional insights on how innovation worked, or didn't work, with all of our clients. Lo and behold, the same patterns emerged. CEOs who held a passion for innovation and conveyed it were experiencing a steady stream of innovation successes. Although they also had some failures, they enjoyed many big successes.

CEOs Alone Are Not at Fault

In no way do all the problems with innovation reside with the CEO. As a CEO myself, I recognize that leadership is definitely a two-way street. You can't effectively lead innovation or create the needed mindset unless you have people who want to make innovation happen. The team has to have a willingness, desire, and passion for innovation. Some people just don't get it and never will, regardless of how effective the CEO is as an innovation leader. People need an instinct for innovation.

Over the years, I've noticed that to be successful at developing new products, each innovation team member should:

1. Have a diversity of experiences (Renaissance person)
2. Be relentlessly optimistic
3. Have a healthy dose of self-confidence, which tends to propel greater creativity
4. Have a propensity toward and be interested in problem solving
5. Like people and convey it effectively

6. Get a rush from and have an intrinsic passion for creating newness

7. Gain a sense of accomplishment from innovating new ideas and launching new products

8. Have experienced failure and have the ability to rise above it

So you need the right cadre of people focused on and dedicated to innovation, along with the right CEO, who's committed to building a culture that will nurture an innovation mindset.

Many managers believe that new products people burn out after 4–5 years. They think that their creativity dries up and their energy dissipates. Does a well-known artist burn out after five years? Ten years? Or even after 30 years? I don't think so! Ed Paschke, the well-known abstract expressionist artist, has been painting for more than 30 years, and he continues to generate new works that build on his previous accomplishments. Likewise, the manager with an innovation mindset is able to think creatively and continues to generate new ways to solve problems throughout his or her life.

Dipping people into new product development for 4–5 years must stop. Innovation requires its own functional area, dedicated people, and consistent funding that won't be arbitrarily cut after a quarterly earnings downturn. Similar to the artist who paints *for life,* innovators need to create *for life.* To achieve this, each must first develop an innovation mindset.

for further reading

Albala, Americo, and Albert H. Rubenstein. "Significant Issues for the Future of Product Innovation: The Coming Revolution in Latin America; The Urgent Need for Explicit Technology Policies/Strategies in the Firm." *Journal of Product Innovation Management* 11 (2) (March 1994): 156–161.

Barrier, Michael. "Innovation as a Way of Life." *Nation's Business* 82 (7) (July 1994): 18–25.

Biemans, Wim G. *Managing Innovation Within Networks.* New York: Routledge, 1992. (ISBN 0415062748)

Calantone, Roger J., and C. Anthony de Benedetto. *Successful Industrial Product Innovation: An Integrative Literature Review.* New York: Greenwood Press, 1990. (ISBN 0313275718)

Chaney, Paul K., Timothy M. Devinney, and Russell S. Winer. "The Impact of New Product Introductions on the Market Value of Firms." *Journal of Business* 64 (4) (October 1991): 573–610.

Collier, Abram T. "Business Leadership and a Creative Society." *Harvard Business Review* 31 (January 1953): 29–38.

Day, George S., Bela Gold, and Thomas D. Kuczmarski. "Significant Issues for the Future of Product Innovation." *Journal of Product Innovation Management* 11 (1) (January 1994): 69–75.

Dobrzynski, Judith. "Annual Meetings Don't Have to Be a Waste of Everybody's Time." *Business Week* (May 10, 1993): 30.

Franck, Frederick. *The Zen of Seeing: Seeing, Drawing as Meditation.* New York: Knopf, 1973. (ISBN 0394488040)

Gilbert, Joseph T. "Choosing an Innovation Strategy: Theory and Practice." *Business Horizons* 6 (November/December 1994): 16–22.

Gruenwald, George. *New Product Development* (videorecording). Lincolnwood, Ill.: NTC Business Video, 1989. (52 min.) (ISBN 0844233501)

Hitt, Michael, Robert E. Hoskisson, and R. Duane Ireland. "A Mid-Range Theory of the Interactive Effects of International and Product Diversification on Innovation and Performance." *Journal of Management* 20 (2) (Summer 1994): 297–326.

Jacobs, Michael T. *Break the Wall Street Rule: Outperform the Stock Market by Investing as an Owner.* Reading, Mass.: Addison-Wesley, 1993. (ISBN 0201632810)

Kanter, Rosabeth Moss. "From the Editor: Ourselves against Ourselves." *Harvard Business Review* 70 (3) (May/June 1992): 8, 10.

Kuczmarski, Susan Smith, and Thomas D. Kuczmarski. *Values-Based Leadership: Rebuilding Employee Commitment, Performance and Productivity.* Englewood Cliffs, N.J.: Prentice Hall, 1995. (ISBN 0131218565)

Kuczmarski, Thomas D. *Managing New Products: The Power of Innovation.* Englewood Cliffs, N.J.: Prentice Hall, 1992. (ISBN 0135446694)

————. "Screening Potential New Products." *Planning Review* 20 (4) (July/August 1992): 24–31, 48.

————, and Arthur G. Middlebrooks. "Innovation Risk & Reward." *Sales & Marketing Management* 145 (2) (February 1993): 44–50.

————. "Inspiring and Implementing the Innovation Mind-Set." *Planning Review* 22 (5) (September/October 1994): 37–38.

LeFavve, Richard G., and Arnoldo C. Hax. "Managerial and Technological Innovations at Saturn Corporation." *MIT Management* (1992).

Miller, Roger. "Global R&D Networks and Large-Scale Innovations: The Case of the Automobile Industry." *Research Policy* 23 (1) (January 1994): 27–46.

New Product Success Stories: Lessons from Leading Innovators. Ed. Robert J. Thomas. New York: John Wiley, 1995. (ISBN 047101320X)

Pakes, Ariel. "On Patents, R&D, and the Stock Market Rate of Return." *Journal of Political Economy* 93 (2) (April 1985): 390–409.

Parsons, Andrew J. "Building Innovativeness in Large U.S. Corporations." *Journal of Services Marketing* 5 (4) (Fall 1991): 5–20.

Patterson, Marvin L., with Sam Lightman. *Accelerating Innovation: Improving the Process of Product Development.* New York: Van Nostrand Reinhold, 1993. (ISBN 0442013787)

Ram, S. (Sundaresan), and Sudha Ram. *A Knowledge-Based Approach for Screening Product Innovations.* Cambridge, Mass.: Marketing Science Institute, 1993.

Rosenberg, DeAnne. "Where Does the Passion Go?" *Industry Week* 241 (16) (August 17, 1992): 11–12.

Shipper, Frank, and Charles C. Manz. "Employee Self-Management Without Formally Designated Teams: An Alternative Road to Empowerment." *Organizational Dynamics* 20 (3) (Winter 1992): 48–61.

Technology Management: Case Studies in Innovation. Ed. Robert Szakonyi. Boston, Mass.: Auerbach, 1992. (ISBN 0791311279)

Terkel, M. *Integrative Management, Innovation, and New Venturing: A Guide to Sustained Profitability.* New York: Elsevier, 1991. (ISBN 0444874445)

West, Alan. *Innovation Strategy.* New York: Prentice Hall, 1992. (ISBN 0134653602)

Zangwill, Willard I. *Lightning Strategies for Innovation: How the World's Best Firms Create New Products.* New York: Lexington Books, 1993. (ISBN 002935675X)

index